Cloister Talks

Cloister Talks

Learning from My Friends the Monks

Jon M. Sweeney

Brazos Press
a division of Baker Publishing Group
Grand Rapids, Michigan

Published by Brazos Press
a division of Baker Publishing Group
P.O. Box 6287, Grand Rapids, MI 49516-6287
www.brazospress.com

Printed in the United States of America

Library of Congress Cataloging-in-Publication Data
Sweeney, Jon M., 1967–
    Cloister talks : learning from my friends the monks / Jon Sweeney.
      p.   cm.
    Includes bibliographical references (p.).
    ISBN 978-1-58743-268-2 (pbk.)
    1. Monastic and religious life. 2. Spirituality—Catholic Church. 3. Spiritual life—Catholic Church. I. Title.
BX2435.S94 2009
248.4′82—dc22   2008054797

All scripture quotations are taken from the New Revised Standard Version and used with permission, with the exception of quotations from the Psalms, which come from the translation in the Book of Common Prayer.

This book is dedicated to the men it describes, the men who have taught me how best to live. Even though I am not one of them, they make me feel as if I am. Nothing in my life, save watching my children grow into adulthood, is sweeter than this feeling.

There is an old Cistercian tradition that a monk is never to be photographed. If he is photographed, he should be unrecognizable. In honor of this tradition and in the spirit of namelessness that endures even now in Trappist life, I have retained only five names of monastics: Thomas Merton, whom I did not know personally; Father Thomas Keating, whom I have met, and whose spirit, stories, and teaching permeate all of Trappist life in America today; M. Basil Pennington, who was my friend, and who died in 2005; Brother Leonard, whose writings I read before his death; and Brother Wayne Teasdale, a friend, who was not a Trappist but whose life was changed when he visited St. Joseph's Abbey in Massachusetts and was befriended by Abbot Thomas Keating and other monks. Wayne took his vows with the Benedictine Bede Griffiths and was living as a "monk in the world" until his death in 2004. The rest of these men will do their best work anon.

CONTENTS

1

CHANGING MY PERCEPTIONS

to change
"place open hands in front of the chest with palms facing inward, then pass one over the other alternately"
—*A Dictionary of the Cistercian Sign Language*

It is 1985 in the flat, lush suburbs west of Chicago. I am graduating from high school. The long lawn of tall oak trees at the front of campus is outfitted with white foldable chairs brought in by a tractor-trailer. I watch on a Friday afternoon as the truck backs in slowly from the state highway, rear first, and men in blue uniforms unload stacks upon stacks of white chairs. By Saturday morning, the chairs sit neatly in their rows—rows that are so snug and so long as to make it awkward to maneuver into an empty seat if you arrive late.

"Excuse me. Excuse me. Pardon me; I'm sorry; excuse me. Oops, sorry about that. Excuse me." I heard these phrases repeated from my place up front with the others in caps and gowns.

The commencement speaker—I don't remember his or her name—said nothing that day that remained with me for more than a few minutes. I took very few photographs when the ceremony was over. There's one of me with a former girlfriend, another with a friend, and one with my mother and father. I remember two things from that afternoon: the sunshine beaming through the large oak trees as I walked across the stage fearing that I'd trip and make a fool of myself, and my thoughts about what I was going to do with my life.

"I hear that you're going to Moody," the father of one of my friends asks me after the service. We are holding those plastic punch cups with the finger holes that are always too small for fingers.

"Yes, that's right, Mr. Thompson," I reply.

"And then what, Jon?"

"I don't know," I said, disingenuously.

I went to Bible college thinking that I was going to become a heroic missionary to the Far East or a preacher who packs in the crowds at a downtown church—crowds like those I had enthusiastically been a part of for my eighteen years.

⸻

It is the hot summer of 1986—hot, that is, in the Philippines, where I was serving as a missionary in the province of Batangas, south of Manila. Having finished my first and only year at Bible college, I was supposed to be working hard to convert Filipino Catholics into Conservative Baptists. Instead I had become interested in Catholic spirituality. My suitcase

Cistercian Sign Language

Trappists still live by a principle of silence, although it is not as strict as it once was. The young Thomas Merton wrote with enthusiasm for the austerities of silence in the 1940s: "Life in these monasteries is austere. In fact, when you compare it with the way people live in the world outside, the austerity is fantastic."[1] Centuries earlier, Cistercian monks developed a sign language all their own, derived from practices in other monastic orders, using hand signs in place of words in both formal and more casual situations. "Eat" was demonstrated by pretending to place something in your mouth. "Mass," by the priestly gesture of breaking the bread. And more mundane, a brother would ask another brother if he wanted coffee by placing the first two fingers of the right hand onto the wrist of the left hand, as if he was checking his pulse. Other excerpts of Cistercian sign language may be found at the heading of each chapter in this book.[2]

had been inordinately heavy as I hauled it off the luggage rack at the airport in Manila in the middle of May. This was long before the days of tight restrictions on the weight of checked baggage. I had packed my bags full of books, including the holy grails of my Bible college days: *The Ryrie Study Bible* and my one-volume *Matthew Henry Commentary*. I'd also brought several books by Catholic authors Thomas Merton and Henri Nouwen.

I wouldn't have known what to say to a monk if I had actually met one in 1986, but they intrigued me. As a child growing up in a conservative evangelical church, a Catholic monk looked the same to me as a Buddhist monk or a Hare Krishna devotee: guys in robes who were probably going to hell.

Merton began to change all of that for me when I first started reading his books in high school. In the Philippines, I read his memoir, *The Seven Storey Mountain*. He made

11

a young monk seem very much like me: confused, uncertain about the future and about God's will, a man seeking a vocation.

By the fall of 1987 I am settled into a liberal arts college back in the Midwest and my missionary goals feel almost as remote to me as elementary school. A Protestant friend— my friends were all Protestant back then—suggests one day as we are leaving history of philosophy class that I visit a monastery.

"You talk about Thomas Merton all the time. Have you ever actually met a monk? Have you ever been to a monastery?"

"No I haven't. I suppose I should. I've thought about it," I say. "In fact, I've been thinking about going to seminary in Louisville, Kentucky, or at least checking it out, and that's not far from Merton's old monastery," I told him.

I simply dropped in on that first occasion. I brought a friend along, a Presbyterian pastor's kid who had likewise never met a monk. Spring break for normal college students means fun in the sun, or sin in Florida. But for Kristin and me, it meant a road trip from Chicago to Kentucky in search of real monks. We were mostly curious about what we'd find. I imagined we would peek through cracks in the walls and see hooded figures performing clandestine ceremonies.

The rolling Knob Hills felt like home. "Just leave me here," I joked to Kristin when we arrived at the Abbey gate. Despite the joke, she was a young woman, and young women are not usually supposed to be wandering around monastery grounds. Frankly, I wasn't supposed to be, either. Crunching acorns underfoot, I wander outside of the retreat house and the first things I notice are orderly white rows of crosses in what turns out to be the graveyard for the members of the community. Merton's grave was in one of those rows, as were a lot of others with names I did not know. I think to myself, *They look a lot like the folding chairs at high school graduation.*

Young men make big mistakes sometimes. They fall in love for the wrong reasons. They drive too fast, usually not because they are late for an important appointment, but because they are playing with the feelings of power inside themselves. They go to war because the sign-up bonus will pay off their credit card debt. They choose careers that will make them look good to their friends, or their parents' friends. We make big mistakes—that's unavoidable. Sometimes I wonder if our lives are marked not by how many *right* decisions we've made, but by how well, quickly, or thoroughly we learn that we have mis-stepped.

I will always wonder if I made a mistake by not becoming a monk when I was twenty years old. I took three trips back and forth to Kentucky that year, in and out of Thomas Merton's old monastery. I talked with the brothers and I sat in church. I prayed and I listened for God's voice. I wasn't Catholic and so never took part in the Eucharistic portions of the services, but the life felt like it could be authentically mine.

"It's just part of my figuring out who I am and what I'm supposed to do," I explained one evening to David, downplaying how important it felt to me. The Mexican restaurant where David and I worked was located in a shopping mall and was packed on this December evening. If I'd had a dollar for every time someone asked me, "Could I get some more chips and salsa?" I'd have been rich.

We should have been paying more attention to our tables, but it was hard to care too deeply about chimichangas and flautas, with or without guacamole, when I was trying to make such a serious decision.

"But don't you feel out of place when you're there? You aren't even Catholic," he said. "And what about your parents, your fiancée, your friends? No one you know is even Catholic, right? It's as if this little dream of yours is not a part of your real life," David said.

He's right, I thought to myself later. *I should be responsible and get married and begin the sort of life that I know best. That's what God wants for me. All of this other stuff is probably me trying to avoid what I'm really supposed to do.*

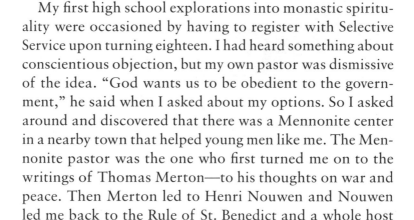

My first high school explorations into monastic spirituality were occasioned by having to register with Selective Service upon turning eighteen. I had heard something about conscientious objection, but my own pastor was dismissive of the idea. "God wants us to be obedient to the government," he said when I asked about my options. So I asked around and discovered that there was a Mennonite center in a nearby town that helped young men like me. The Mennonite pastor was the one who first turned me on to the writings of Thomas Merton—to his thoughts on war and peace. Then Merton led to Henri Nouwen and Nouwen led me back to the Rule of St. Benedict and a whole host of other things. After a few years of this, I simply had to see for myself.

Ever since those days, I have had moments of yearning for a monastic life, even amid my own very busy "secular" life. And when I began to get to know actual monks, I realized that questions of identity and belonging are never entirely settled.

"There have been plenty of times when I've wondered what my life would have been like if I had never come here," Father Ambrose told me one day as we strolled around the church of his monastery. Father Ambrose had entered Merton's Abbey of Gethsemani in the early 1950s. "Don't worry about those sorts of doubts and questions. They mean that you are still alive!" he said with a serious laugh.

Over the two decades since those early explorations, there have been times when I didn't go on retreat as planned because I wasn't sure if I'd want to come back at the end. On one occasion I cancelled a plane reservation the day before I was supposed to fly down to a monastery in Georgia. On another occasion, I spent Christmas morning with a group of Benedictine monks in Vermont about an hour and a half from home while my wife and kids waited patiently for my return so that we could begin opening presents.

On one other occasion, my wife and I decided to take a road trip to Nashville to see family and then on to Memphis to see Graceland. (My daughter was in a retro crazy-for-Elvis phase.) On the return trip, I charted a course through Kentucky because I wanted to see those Knob Hills once more. "I'd love to just spend a couple of hours at the Abbey of Gethsemani, if you don't mind," I said to my wife. She was understanding, but I don't think she actually understood. In a downpour, she and the kids dropped me at the Abbey gate and then they went for ice cream. I sat down with Brother Michael, who had been one of Merton's closest friends, and we talked for about two hours. Through all of these experiences, I tried to feed my two desires at the same time, and it never quite worked. I didn't know how to incorporate it all together.

I continued to read a lot of Merton throughout my first decade of married life. His books fed me more than any other author, I'm sure. But they have infuriated me at times too. In my late twenties, when all I could think about were the worries of making rent, my young wife who seemed to be ill much of the time, and wanting my young children to be healthy and safe, Merton's talk about living a quiet, contemplative life made me angry. How dare he, or anyone else, paint a picture of a carefree, intimate kind of living with God that was unavailable to someone in the midst of a life like mine! Once drawn to the monastery, now I felt as far from its comforts and promises as a man could possibly feel. I had to put my Merton books away for several years.

"Why do you keep going to those places," my friend James scolded me one afternoon as we left work about eight years ago. It was late in December around 5 p.m. and already as dark as a cave in northern New England. We walked into the dimly lit parking lot searching for our cars. Snow was falling gently.

"Don't you think that you might be wasting your time, Jon?" James asked, scraping some ice from his windshield.

I had just returned from another weekend retreat to Our Lady of the Holy Spirit Monastery in Conyers, Georgia, and the last thing on my mind was that I might be wasting my time. Nevertheless, having visited monasteries for many years, I wasn't quite sure exactly what I *was* doing. I was in my thirties, still feeling like I hadn't figured out who I was.

James was one of the only good friends I'd made since moving to Vermont a few years earlier. I confided in him from time to time and on this occasion he was on to something. James knew that for years I had been searching for spiritual adventure, vaguely dissatisfied with what I had at home and in church. I sought out beautiful vistas, the most unusual, intriguing, or ascetical teachers, and did my share of spiritual experimentation.

Each intriguing ascetic would say quixotic things to me and my mind would almost literally pop with excitement. I would run home and for a week be obsessed with the idea, *Now that just might be the key to my life! He might have the answers!* I would think for the umpteenth time.

Then I would buy all of the teacher's books or tapes and the books that he recommended. And I'd read them—or at least the first few pages of them. This may be familiar to you too. Many of my books have lonely bookmarks on about page twelve! At about that point in the book I'd begin wondering, *Why was I all excited about this?*

Monasteries are places where I would often hear someone say something that spoke directly to my heart—a teaching or a word of guidance that would somehow make the different pieces of my life seem to fit together. Between visits to monasteries I would listen to cassette tapes of the talks given by Merton when he was a novice master in the 1950s and early 1960s. Each tape was the perfect length to accompany me on a walk or in the bath or on my way to work, the occasions when I would get away alone and think. I knew some of those tapes almost by heart.

But the retreat I had just taken changed my life forever. I remember moving quickly with Father Ambrose, trying to keep up with him both on foot and in conversation. Ambrose had made his original solemn vows in Kentucky, but then became one of the founding monks of the Georgia abbey in the 1950s. He had been in Georgia for more than fifty years by the time we first met. Ambrose was a priest (not all monks are priests), but also something of a handyman. He had fixed just about everything that could be fixed around the monastery, including the elevator and the wiring of the retreat house.

We took a walk around the lake one morning after breakfast. The cicadas, the crickets, even the frogs were quiet on that December morning.

"I have a bit of free time. Let's go before the abbot comes up with something for me to do!" he said with a laugh and a twinkle in his eye.

The grounds are unremarkable in winter; no snow, not in Georgia, but every living thing seems to sit in silence, hidden from sight. I couldn't wait to get him talking. "I never want to leave when I'm in a place like this, with people like you, and yet, I love my wife and family and even my work very much. What do you think that means?" I asked.

He shrugged and he smiled. We walked a little farther.

I went on. "What should I be looking for and listening for, I mean, when I come to the monastery? Whatever I'm finding now—in the way I'm doing it now—seems to inspire me at the time but only confuse me later," I explained.

Still, Ambrose was quiet. We walked on for another minute or two until we came to a bench under a tree. We sat down. Ambrose stopped and looked at me for what seemed like a minute but was probably more like ten seconds. He crossed his long legs from one side to the other—almost imperceptible in his black gown—as a way of emphasizing a point, and he said, "Busy people like you come here all the time. I see them in church, in the retreat house, and walking around the grounds. You come here to slow down, we know that."

"Sometimes I give talks to the retreatants," he went on, "and sometimes I give retreats for Protestant ministers. You're all busy people, of course."

Ambrose has such an interesting mind. When he talks it's as if he's painting the circles on a target, beginning at the outer ones. "If I had to give you one piece of advice it would be this: don't look for sudden enlightenment. People call them ah-ha moments; don't worry about those. I know that you may feel your time is wasted here if you haven't had enough ah-has, but I assure you it won't be."

"So what should I be doing?" I asked him, feeling confused and more than a little bit foolish.

"When you finally quiet down enough you'll begin to hear a splinter of the divine voice."

I discovered before long that Ambrose often mixed his metaphors, but I think I understood.

"When you visit here, don't walk around looking for moments of enlightened insight," Ambrose advised me. "For one thing, we're not that smart!" He laughed. "Instead, you should walk around praying. Sit in the church before dawn, praying. Or just shut your mouth for a few days. Listen to the talks given by the retreat master, if you like. Just sit. Try your best to stop thinking."

It sounded too easy to me. I told him that.

"What I'm suggesting is much harder than you might think. You'll see."

At that point, I felt the need to lighten things up. "What about a little old-fashioned scourging? Wouldn't that be easier?"

"Yes, well," he said, smiling, "we Trappists aren't much into asceticism anymore. Beating yourself up doesn't do for you what the monks of earlier centuries thought it would do: purify you. In fact, it only confuses things further," he explained, as if he knew whereof he spoke. He was a monk who had started out long before the reforms of the Second Vatican Council. He used to sleep on a wooden plank in winter in a mostly unheated dormitory.

"So, here's your ascetical work for this week: Try your best not to be clever or insightful. Try your best not to look in the mirror. Don't think much about combing your hair or whatever image you want to show to the world. Think of this time as a stripping away of paint to reveal what's underneath.

"If you're lucky, you'll uncover some of your truer self before you leave—and it will change you, or stick with you much better than an ah-ha ever could," Ambrose concluded.

He was right.

⸎

More than twenty years after my college flirtations with the idea of taking vows of celibacy, stability, and obedience, I'm still drawn to the monastic life. I know now that those feelings were not infatuation, but truly some sort of real love that continues to be elusive, but also one of the most important parts of my life. The wisdom of contemporary, contemplative monasticism has been my greatest source of guidance for how to be a secular (non-monastic) Christian.

I have learned so much from the monastics that I feel the need to sit down and try and distill it. I have found that the best way to communicate their wisdom is through stories, episodes, and portions of conversations that have happened on quiet afternoons in the monastery or while walking together outside: cloister talks.

I visit monasteries today and talk with monks from a whole different perspective from the one I had when I was younger. I'm still seeking something—I'll always feel like I'm seeking more wisdom, more understanding, truer love, a clearer way of hearing the voice of God—but now my jittery heart has settled down.

2

THE WAY OF THE CAMEL

heart
"with tips of both forefingers draw a heart over the heart"
—*A Dictionary of the Cistercian Sign Language*

Father Ambrose's message on that December day changed my perspective on a whole lot of things. His words were like an insight to end other insights.

A monk is the sort of man I want to be, though I live outside the cloister. I enjoy these guys because their way of life makes it possible to take a longer view of things. They easily discuss the *big questions* without becoming occupied with them. They ponder without too much deducing. They pray without talking too much. They adore God without falling asleep. These are all skills I don't naturally possess but would love to learn.

They also have a way of religious speak that avoids jargon. In every religious community or environment that I've been a part of, there's a jargon, and I easily get caught up in it. There's evangelical-speak, liberal Christian-speak, emerging-speak, peace-and-justice-speak, and it's all very tiring and meaningless after awhile. I find that monks somehow avoid all of this. Perhaps it is because they take the time to listen and so they then speak more clearly and plainly.

"What you are doing may be important stuff, but it's who you are that God wants to know," Father Ambrose advised me one day. "Talk less and think less, Jon," he said. This sounded a bit like the advice a corporate executive once gave my brother when he was trying to go to graduate school, be married, and work all at the same time. "Get less sleep!" he advised Doug— and he was serious. Ambrose was serious too.

Think less. Speak less. Do less. Try to be less. Why on earth would that be good for me? I wondered. But only until I began to take his advice. What a change it made in my life! In the old days I would prepare a to-do list and a list of goals before leaving for a monastery visit. My lists would be on the opening pages of a flip notebook, like this:

1. Pack lightly and unpack quickly upon arrival.
2. Kneel down at foot of bed and pray for a good retreat.
3. On day one, get up early enough to make 4 a.m. Vigils.
4. Don't miss a Compline service.
5. Centering prayer twice a day for 20 minutes.
6. Pray while walking.

My over-seriousness was often masked as healthy preparation, but in truth, it was a way of not allowing God's grace to function. I laugh at this now, because these days when I go on retreat I do almost the opposite: my goal is to live, at least for a time, as if I don't have goals to achieve.

───── ∞ ─────

There is something reassuring about the thick stone walls of a monastery. The physical sturdiness of the place reinforces the ancient practices and teachings that you encounter inside. To sit in an abbey church and pray along with the brothers, or to listen to a chapter talk, is to do something Christians have done since the first hermits began to gather in communities outside the major city centers of Egypt, Palestine, and Syria. A man in Alexandria, Jerusalem, or Antioch must have grown tired of his day job and domestic responsibilities; he must have wondered how to deepen his spiritual life beyond sitting in church once a week. And so he rode. He rode a camel out to where the monks had set up their communities.

That's what I do now: I ride my metaphorical camel to see the men in the monastery from time to time. These men live their lives in out-of-the-way places. You would never meet them unless you set out to find them—and I've been blessed by finding them. They live in stone houses at the end of long roads, and my camel journeys are always rewarding.

Monks prefer anonymity and live by it in subtle ways. When I once tried to draw a Trappist acquaintance out to talk, he replied he was a simple monk without desire for notice of any kind. He told me that, at seventy-some years old and suffering from Lou Gehrig's disease, he would be dead soon, and he had instructed his brothers at the abbey to bury him as quietly as possible without any notice whatever. "Lay brothers tend to be very reserved and shun publicity. For thirteen years I lived somewhat as a hermit here on the property. There is even a note in my personnel file requesting a simple Latin/English death notice rather than one with a picture and a 'blurb,'" he wrote me in a letter. That was four years ago; he's gone now.

On the other hand, I have met many monks who love to talk. You'd never know that some of them once lived by rules of silence in and around the abbey. Known for their faithfulness to the letter of the Rule of St. Benedict, Trappists were once religious about silence. St. Benedict wrote: "If we should sometimes for the sake of the virtue of silence refrain even from good conversation, we should all the more, for fear of the penalty of sin, refrain from evil words."[1] Up until the 1960s, silence was not so much the environment as it was the rule in a Cistercian abbey. Those rules vanished along with a bunch of others at the time of the Second Vatican Council.

Many monks are so full of life that conversation seems, at times, to burst out when they know that the person before them is anxious to listen. I'm all ears when I'm with them, and they know it.

Father Luke of St. Joseph's Abbey in Massachusetts is one of the most endearing monks I have known. He and I forged a strong bond over the years. He's a short man with a lot of energy. In the hood of his cowl, his neck almost disappears, making him look cozy. Luke is always seeing the lighter side of the more serious rules in the monastery. About Trappist silence, he once told me the following story: "As a young monk, I was always messing around in the refectory, the infirmary, even sometimes, I'm sorry to admit, in church. We used to accuse each other of our sins, you know. It was a serious affair, or at least was always intended to be serious. I was often accused of making useless hand signs. I would actually cultivate this *sin* because it made the other men laugh. Not talking became an opportunity for lightheartedness. My favorite memory of frivolous signs was the one that I once made urgently to the priest who was celebrating at the altar, 'There's not enough wine!' I signed to him during the Mass. I was kidding, of course—well, in retrospect, perhaps that wasn't such a good idea!" And Luke let out a laugh.

Father Luke talks about his faults and past sins with a certain ease that I don't often find in other people. Somewhere in one of his novels, Graham Greene says that murderers are probably the most loquacious of people. You could say that only great sinners have a lot to say about what they've done wrong, but I don't think that's quite it with monks. They talk a lot about their sins not because they have sinned more than the average person—I've found very few monks with exciting pre-conversion stories—but rather because they know what sin is. Without the din of the world, they are more sensitive. With hourly prayers and liturgy, a monk's life easily fits into God's narrative. They feel sin, or experience it, more thoroughly, and then they experience God's forgiveness more keenly too.

⸺⸺❀⸺⸺

On a rainy afternoon in early February, I drove down from Vermont to see Father Luke. We were supposed to have met three days earlier, but I cancelled with an early morning e-mail saying that I should stay off the roads due to freezing rain. So we rescheduled. When it began to rain again on the Tuesday morning three days later, with a temperature hovering just above freezing, I was determined to stick to the plan. I drove down without incident on what happened to be Shrove Tuesday.

Father Luke was recovering from a bout of pneumonia, I discovered when I arrived, but his spirits were bright. I asked if Shrove Tuesday meals were planned for the monastery.

"Oh yes, it's pizza night!" he said with enthusiasm. "There will be many, many pizzas. We will eat our fill."

I laughed. The image of monks answering the door for the Domino's pizza delivery kid, his car radio blaring behind him as he handed over a stack of pizzas, struck me as hilarious.

"Are you ordering out?" I asked with a smile.

"No, no," Luke said. "I just saw the cook and his two assistants in the kitchen a few minutes ago. They have been chopping mushrooms all morning."

"Will there be any meat on any of those pizzas?"

"No, never meat, even on Shrove Tuesday. We're pretty traditional in that regard," Luke said. "Some of the monasteries now have turkey on Thanksgiving, but we don't do that. You only have occasional meat in the infirmary."

I had heard that before: meat and eggs mostly in the infirmary, an ancient monastic tradition of helping the sick to become well. But on this afternoon, I had a lot of questions to ask, and so I tried to change the subject. Despite his advanced age, I am always delighted at how Father Luke is able to quickly move from one topic to the next, without missing a beat. Pizzas one minute and salvation the next.

"What can I do for you, today?" Luke looked me in the eye.

"Give me perspective," I replied, ready for it.

"That's good," he said. "I think we're good at that. But perspective on what, exactly?"

Some people climb mountains. Some people challenge themselves with enormous tasks that seem impossible to accomplish. Some overwork themselves. Others fuss endlessly over details. Others find their greatest joy in traveling to big cities and having new experiences. We all try to fill our lives with meaning. Some of all of those things appeal to me too, but recently I've learned that my greatest joy comes in simplifying. I take pleasure in having and doing very little. Or throwing stuff away. Not having to do anything or be anything. Not being aloof, but being alone. I explained this in some jumbled way to Luke.

"You are beginning to sound like a monk," he said. "You're learning." A smile spread across my face.

If you've never had the experience of leaving behind your laptop, cell phone, Blackberry, pager, and life's usual commitments for a few days at a monastery—you should. Turning my communication devices off for even a half-day at a time has fed my soul, but a long weekend or week is best of all. I sometimes get to the point, after a day or two, when I only turn my cell phone on once a day to see if I have messages. That's usually about the best I can manage.

When I go on retreat, the first day is usually a time for sleep. By day two, I am able to enter into the prayer and liturgical life of the monastery and I begin spending time in the church from 4 a.m. until the most beautiful hour, Compline, at about 8 p.m. Then, by day three, I find myself able to listen to what I normally can't hear: those interior voices of both good and bad that are silenced in my secular life. One of the great teachers of Christian mysticism wrote: "God, the Divine Spirit, is indeed before, within, and after all our truest dignity *and deepest disquiet.*"[2] My head gets very noisy before it is able to quiet down.

That Shrove Tuesday afternoon I asked Father Luke, "Is it normal for my mind to be spinning with concerns at the precise time I am supposed to be quieting down?"

"Yes, I hear that a lot from people," he said. "It takes time, and patience."

Being a Trappist monk must be an odd vocation. By principle, he is not supposed to become a scholar or specialist, not a great preacher or poet, not even a theologian. Still, I know many of them who would agree with Dante that theology is the "bread of angels," and with Tevye (from *The Fiddler on the Roof*) that they'd rather discuss the holy books than do manual work. A contemplative is hard to define, but it is relatively clear what they do.

I remember the first time I visited with Brother Wayne Teasdale in the late 1990s. Wayne was a long-time monastic and a friend of many Trappists who had lived in cloistered communities on at least two continents. Toward what turned out to be the end of his life Wayne was living as a self-described "monk in the world" in the inner city of Chicago's south side. He was teaching at a seminary, involved in a variety of causes, but most of all he was an enthusiast for silent, contemplative prayer even beyond the typical Trappist.

I had been taught centering prayer on a couple of occasions over the years, and I had tried it off and on from time to time, but I was still a complete novice. For Brother Wayne, this was the foundation of his life. He corresponded with people in need—men in prison, small religious communities in countries like China and Myanmar that were fighting for their right to live and worship in peace—and the strength for this work, he said, all came from his connection to God in prayer.

We first met on a sunny morning in late May. I was in town for a conference and unfortunately wearing my coat and tie when he greeted me at his apartment door. *I don't want him to think that clothes like these define me*, I remember thinking. *I'm sure he thinks I'm too corporate.*

Wayne and I sat down in his living room on old couches and chatted for a few minutes. He asked me about my work. I asked him about his work. I asked him about his health; I had heard that he had some form of cancer. I found the intensity of his gaze a bit unnerving. He seemed to be very *present*.

And then he asked, "Do you pray much, Jon?"

Perhaps for a monk this sort of question is commonplace, but it seemed abrupt and not a little bit rude.

"Well, yes," I replied, uncertainly.

Wayne quickly added, "Great, then let's spend some time in prayer together. How about forty-five minutes or so? Can you spare that long?" It occurred to me: this was how he made friends.

"Yeah, sure," I said, scared to death at the idea of sitting in a quiet room without any other stimulant whatever for most of an hour. I hadn't exactly been forthcoming about my prayer experience.

We sat down in a couple of chairs and he set an alarm clock to beep at the appointed time. *Forty-five minutes!* I thought I was going to jump out of my skin.

The first five minutes felt like a half an hour, and by what I imagined was the midway point I began trying to remember each offensive position player on the 1985 Chicago Bears, simply to avoid screaming out loud. *Wide receivers . . . Willie Gault, Dennis McKinnon, Kevin Margarum. Let's see, the offensive line was Jay Hilgenberg, Keith Van Horn . . .*

Finally, I lied at the end.

"That was terrific," I said, when he asked me if I enjoyed our time together, wondering, *Could he tell from the look on my face that I didn't actually do it?*

Leaving Wayne, straightening my coat and tie on my way down the hall, I couldn't help wondering how many hours he must sit in quiet prayer like that.

———⟨∞⟩———

Being thrown into the deep end of the pool has taught me to swim, but it has also shown me just how fuzzy my perspective was. I usually define and describe my spiritual practices using ideal words rather than real ones and I don't often realize my own fuzziness until I'm talking with one of my monk friends.

It is fairly easy to mean what I say when I say things like one of the Ten Commandments. *I do not commit adultery.* That's fairly simple to accomplish in my life and obviously,

I know if and when I'm accomplishing it. But how much harder it is to mean what I say when I say things that have become formulaic for those of us well-versed in Christian spirituality. I say them so easily: *I grow closer to God each day. To live is Christ, to die is gain. I believe in Jesus Christ, the only Son of God.* Growing up in the church, these affirmations roll off the tongue. It's hard to know when I'm actually meaning them.

"I've noticed that you don't use a lot of the language that I use," I remarked to Father Luke once. We were sitting in comfortable chairs in the living room of the retreat house, talking. A large, oak table stood in the center of the room.

"I suppose that's true," he replied. "Perhaps I don't."

Father Luke mused, "You know, I remember hippie kids sitting at that table studying the Bhagavad-Gita and the New Testament side-by-side. I never see that table getting used today; we always sit around the room's perimeter."

"You need to talk less and listen more," another monk, Brother Samuel, told me later, when I asked him why he rarely used religious language. He too was an old man who had joined his monastery a half century earlier. *I listen*, I thought to myself with silent indignation.

"There's listening and then there's listening," he said, as if he knew what I was thinking. "Too much talk makes for too little listening, and without true listening you will never really know." He concluded his thought, leaving the sentence to dangle in the silence.

―――∞∞∞―――

Whether catching the bus to Conyers, Georgia, flying to Louisville and doing the same to Trappist, Kentucky, or getting in the car and meandering the few hours south to St. Joseph's Abbey outside of Worcester, Massachusetts—nothing seems to happen until I've left the cocoon of what I know. I once sat in my car in the abbey parking lot, on day two of a retreat, just listening to the radio; I was craving information. It was like a withdrawal. I later realized I had to return to the idea of the camel, entering the abbey gates in a way that left me no recourse but to quiet down.

It was March 2001 and I arrived on a Monday evening to meet with Father Ambrose Tuesday morning. I had just woken up a few hours earlier, but he was in midday, wearing his secular work clothes: blue jeans, T-shirt, and an old cap of some sort. He didn't look at all like a monk who had sat in choir singing psalms for a few hours before dawn. Outside, a man with a pickaxe slung over his shoulder was walking toward a shed carrying three orange buckets. Another man walked behind with three more buckets. The monks were at work. *I guess that Ambrose's work is me, today*, I thought to myself.

"I've begun contemplative practice at home and it is very unsettling for me," I explained to Ambrose. "In my centering prayer times, thoughts pop up and ruin everything. I cannot block them out. And then faults of mine come to mind—even problems that I'd managed to forget about seem to creep back in at those moments when I'm trying to be quiet and listen for God. Is that normal?" I asked him.

"Oh, yes," he said, "You're not crazy!" he went on with a laugh. "Even if you have practiced connections to God through scripture study, petitionary prayer, church attendance, care for others—you will still feel unsettled when you begin to quiet down and practice your belief.

"In fact, as St. John of the Cross was fond of pointing out, our feelings of disconcertedness are probably indicators that God is nearby. It's not the other way around. God has to make us more like him, and that leads to some unsettling times, my friend," he concluded.

Ambrose's mind wandered for a minute. He looked out the window. "Flannery O'Connor—do you know her, the Catholic writer from very near these parts? She wrote often about the unsettling nature of true religion. Anyway, I remember one of her letters talking about how unlike a comfy blanket true religion is. Look it up!" he challenged me. "That's certainly been my experience."

"She also said that 'vocation implies limitation,'" he added.

Father Ambrose, it turns out, had met Flannery O'Connor, who lived most of her life in Milledgeville, Georgia, not far from the monastery in Conyers. And I looked it up: "What people don't realize is how much religion costs. They think faith is a big electric blanket, when of course it is the cross. It is much harder to believe than not to believe," wrote Flannery O'Connor in a letter to Louise Abbot.[3]

⚬⚬⚬

There was a time several years ago when I wanted to maroon myself on a Trappist island somewhere. Work was no longer fun, my kids were having problems in school, and only my spiritual life felt nourishing.

I'd been looking forward to a fresh visit to the Georgia monastery for months, and this time, I'd driven over from Nashville, where I had some appointments for work.

At certain points in my life, the words that come from church pulpits feel empty and the notes of hymns feel like they float out of the building rather than speak to my soul. *If I could only go the monastery, I could be the Christian I am supposed to be*, I often thought. Wasn't it John Wayne who once said in an interview, "I don't much like God when he gets under a roof"?

You have to set your alarm if you want to make it to Lauds in the morning. I always carry my own travel alarm clock, distrusting the alarms on other clocks completely. On morning number one, it worked, as usual, and I was sliding quietly down the side aisle of the abbey church at 3:45 a.m., ready to intone the quiet psalms. In Georgia, the monks have the space and the openness to allow retreatants to sit in the same choir stalls as themselves. I love this. Makes me feel like one of the guys.

There are two remarkable things about Our Lady of the Holy Spirit Monastery. One is the memory of Flannery O'Connor's peacocks that used to walk around outside by the lake. The Catholic novelist willed her famous birds to the monks when she was dying of lupus. And the other is their amazing church. Built of limestone and wood, the church is a mixture of functional construction and beauty of form. The vaulted ceiling of the nave reminds me of European cathedrals,

The Plan of a Trappist Monastery

The layout of a monastery has followed a circumscribed plan from the first ones in the Middle Ages down through the present. The church is the centerpiece of the compound and adjoining it are those places that are usually closed to visitors: the cloisters (covered but open air place for quiet reflection), the refectory (dining room), infirmary, and the dormitories or cells or rooms where the monks sleep. The only real changes in the last century have been driven by changes in how monasteries earn their bread. Livestock and agriculture used to be the primary means of support, and nearly every monastery would have stables, pens for goats, sheep, and pigs, barns, and also occasionally additional dormitories for hired-hand farm workers who would supplement the work of the monks. Nearly every Trappist monastery has downgraded or eliminated livestock and serious agriculture from their way of life, and have instead found new ways of supporting themselves.

or a great Gothic structure such as St. Patrick's Cathedral in New York City, but the indigenous materials of concrete and limestone, not marble or granite, feel at home in what used to be a remote part of Georgia.

The out-of-the-way-ness of a monastery is part of its appeal. Monks live in picturesque places, which helps to convince people like me to visit them. The sunrises can be amazing (Abbey of Gethsemani in Kentucky), the ocean views breathtaking (New Camoldoli Hermitage in Big Sur, California), the native flowers and butterflies intoxicating (Our Lady of the Holy Spirit in Conyers, Georgia), but the reason why most monasteries originally settled in out-of-the-way places was that the land was available and inexpensive. Also, like monks of every era and religious tradition, they wanted to be out of the way.

"A diversion that becomes permanent," Brother Paul once explained. "Not a diversion of location, but a diversion of spirit."

———— ❦ ————

It's not that monks believe cities and suburbs are somehow wrong or unchristian, but contemplative monasteries exist as the antidote to busy, secular lives. It's not that it's wrong to live a busy, secular life (I certainly do), but you're supposed to have more than that, and the more than that is supposed to eventually take prominence.

It isn't easy to get to a monastic location. Pull out a map and check out the winding roads that take you from the city twenty or thirty or a hundred miles out to where the abbey sits in a valley or on a hillside away from most everything else. Unless you drive yourself, the journey may include a plane ride and then more than a taxi from the airport. Usually a long bus ride is followed by one of the hospitable monks picking you up at the station. Just like pilgrimage used to mean in the Middle Ages, your mind and body will travel those final miles in slow motion, as if you are arriving on foot, with your pack slung over your shoulder. When I'm on my way, I feel a lot like those city-dwellers of late antiquity who rode their camels to go find something different.

Father Luke and I sat outside talking at St. Joseph's Abbey one afternoon. The scene could not have been lovelier. We sat in the hot, late October sun, looking at the hillsides that were once farmed by the Trappists of Massachusetts. Pale oranges and pale yellows combined on the horizon like in a Van Gogh painting. Father Luke was reminiscing about our friend, Basil Pennington, and how vigorously he worked in those fields as a young man. Basil has always been the connection point between me and Father Luke. "I must say that it's very hard to be a contemplative in ugliness," he said, finally, with a big smile. "We do love our places."

A Medieval Ditty

Each of the famous religious orders has a founder, and those founders are some of the most important figures in Christian history. The following saying originated sometime in the late Middle Ages, and illustrates the spirit and personality of four of the most popular monastic founders/reformers in history:

> *Bernardus valles,*
> *montes Benedictus amabat,*
> *Franciscus vicos,*
> *celebres Dominicus urbes.*

> Bernard loved the valleys,
> Benedict loved the mountains,
> Francis the villages,
> and Dominic the crowded cities.

There will always be plenty of people who visit monasteries because of their scenic locations. That's not the point, and yet, the monks don't at all mind because they know what can happen once you've arrived.

"Nature is one of the revelations of God," Father Luke said. "After all, you began as a created cell. There's no war between beauty in nature and the appreciation of God."

———————

More than twenty years after I first began spending time with Catholic monks, I still occasionally feel the need to explain to myself and others why these relationships have been so important to me as a Christian and as a man.

I have listened to the monastics with an ear that is mostly Protestant. This comes through, I'm sure, in the sort of questions that I've asked and perhaps even in the ways that I've heard the answers. My background is of the rational sort; I like to explain things at least for myself, and I think that explaining things leads to knowing more about them. But in this process, the monks have shown me again and again that there is much more to be known by the heart than the head, more to be gleaned in the darkness of the abbey church than the bright light of the abbey library. I have listened as the Protestant that I am, but as one who wants to be a little bit more Catholic.[4]

Sometimes I feel the need to apologize for praising monasticism, since some Protestants think of monks as men avoiding real life. It is true that the original ideals of monasticism included avoiding civilization in order to better embrace the divine. One writer accurately captures it this way: "It was a means of escape from a social condition that made spiritual advancement impossible. The essential idea was the saving of the individual soul through renunciation and withdrawal beyond the influences of death-dealing conditions. This was, I think, St. Benedict's original and perhaps sole idea, the establishing of havens of refuge in the midst of social anarchy where those who desired might find and follow the teachings of Christ."[5] Pope Benedict XVI's recent encyclical on hope even addresses this criticism, so it must be that not only Protestants, but some Catholics too, still wonder if there isn't too much avoidance of the real world in the life of a contemplative.

Other times, I find myself running up against my Protestantism while actually in conversation with a monk.

"I am, after all, Protestant," I said, almost apologizing to Father Basil one day over lunch. "I ask all of these questions because most of this is new to me, you see."

We were sitting in an overpass restaurant about five miles outside of Boston. Two weeks beforehand I had seen online that the great preacher, William Sloane Coffin, would be having a public conversation with his friend, the Harvard Divinity School professor, Harvey Cox. Coffin had recently suffered a stroke and this was his first public appearance since the illness. I knew that Cox and Basil were old friends and so I e-mailed Basil at the abbey.

"Did you know that Harvey Cox is doing a public interview of William Sloane Coffin at Andover Newton Seminary two weeks from today? Would you like me to pick you up and drive you into Boston for the afternoon? We could listen to Coffin and Cox, say hello to them, and also get some time in the car to talk about your book." I was one of Basil's editors.

"Yes, I'd love that. Come. And let's get some lunch on the way. I know a good place off the Mass Pike," he wrote back within the hour.

Basil was an enormous man and he loved life like no one else I've known. His love of food was something we shared.

That lunch included appetizers, entrees, and desserts; I was stuffed to the gills by the time we returned to the car and headed toward Andover Newton.

I decided to repeat a criticism that I'd heard from a relative who was concerned about me being so interested in monasticism.

"Have you ever felt as if you are fleeing the world by being a monk? Have you, in some ways, given up responsibility for others by living in a cloister, working on your own salvation?" I winced inside as I said it.

Basil didn't wince. He gestured toward me the way you do with your knuckle when you don't want to be too aggressive by pointing directly at someone. "That doesn't sound like you, Jon. I should ask you, What are *you* running from?

"The essence of the contemplative life, and the monastic life, is to give up yourself completely, to give yourself over completely to God and to others. And regarding salvation— saving yourself is one of the more recent but persistent myths. I'll tell you, it isn't Catholic. Jesus's message was never about saving yourself, but about saving others. We have to be interested in everyone's salvation, not just our own," Basil said.

I'm not the first Protestant to have doubts about monasticism. The late medieval reformer John Wycliffe once said, "A good friar is as rare as a phoenix." And then Martin Luther infamously referred to monks as lice, as instruments of the devil, and where he was able, Luther closed the monasteries in Germany.

Interestingly, Luther was a devout Augustinian monk before the Reformation, one of the *most* devout, according to his own accounting, and there's no reason to doubt him. Perhaps this explains the virulence with which he attacked the institution after he had left it behind. During his battles with the papacy Luther eventually even expanded his initiative to "rescuing" nuns from their convents. The woman who would become Luther's wife was one such nun. She was hidden along with a dozen others in barrels by Luther and his helpers and wheeled out of their Cistercian convent to "freedom."

Why did he oppose monasticism so much? Well, in the late Middle Ages it was presumed that being a monk was a higher spiritual calling and a more direct path to the Divine than could be found in normal, secular life. Also, it was believed that the formal vows of monasticism were like a new baptism, cleansing oneself from all sin in a way that was more efficient than the normal making of confession done by non-monastic Christians.

"Luther was right to protest these things," Basil once told me.

After Luther came a whole host of others who lambasted the idea of running to the cloister and following medieval superstitions. One popular adage during the Renaissance was, "The friar preached against theft, when he had a goose in his sleeve." During the Enlightenment, one of the most popular novels was simply called *The Monk* by Matthew Lewis, an attaché to the British Embassy at the Hague. Its sinister portrayal of the men of a Capuchin monastery in Madrid was both representative of the thinking around 1800, and has been influential in the imaginations of those who do not understand the purpose of becoming a monk ever since.

The secretly sinful monk, the gluttonous friar, the hypocritical monk, and the superstitions of institutional religion that used to hold power over the faithful no longer make sense in our world. My experiences with monks have been of a very different sort. I can't imagine that those stereotyped characters exist any longer. Perhaps this is because the world

Distinguishing between
Benedictine, Cistercian, and Trappist

Benedictines originated with St. Benedict (480–543) in Italy in the early sixth century. Within a few decades of Benedict's death there was a house of monks in nearly every medium-size town in Italy. Their monasteries came to dominate the religious landscape of Europe, and they educated the majority of Europe's political, civic, and religious leaders for centuries. Cistercians (O. Cist.) originated in the early eleventh century, as an attempt to reform lax practices that had grown into Benedictine monasteries. They also sought to recover the Benedictine principle that each monastery was to function as an independent family. By about 1200 AD, there were at least 500 monasteries involved in the Cistercian reforms. Later, in the early seventeenth century came the Trappist reform among the Cistercians. The Trappists were seeking a stricter observance to the original ideals of St. Benedict, following another period of neglect, and came to call themselves the Order of Cistercians of the Strict Observance (O.C.S.O.). Their movement centered in the French monasteries, particularly the one at La Trappe, which is where the *Trappist* name originates. It is the Trappists that most influenced Cistercian life in North America, where today there exist many more O.C.S.O. Cistercian monasteries (16) than those of the O. Cist. (2).

has changed a great deal in the last 200 years. We live in a time when not only has religion lost its powerful hold over people's lives, but monks are among the most powerless.

⁂

"What are you running from?" Basil had asked me.

"I don't know," I told him. "Or, I mean, I didn't know that I was."

A year later, I was talking with Father Luke. "Let me suggest an alternative to your spirituality," he said. Luke had begun using the word *spirituality* in our conversations, probably thinking that it would allow him to relate to me better. "You need the spirituality of dependence."

This didn't make much sense to me at first, because I know my Rule of St. Benedict. When someone comes to the monastery seeking to become a monk, let him knock on the door over and over again, St. Benedict advised. Be uncooperative, he says. In fact, see even if he will put up with unkind replies from the other side of the door, Benedict said.

In *Monty Python and the Holy Grail*, the insults shouted down by the French-accented knights upon the approaching King Arthur and his attendants remind me of this medieval practice. They hilariously shout down insults on the presumptuous Arthur: "Go and boil your bottoms, you sons of a silly person! I blow my nose at you!" "Your mother was a hamster and your father smells of elderberries!"

Benedict advised rebuke, unkindness, uncooperativeness, maybe even insult in order to turn away those who might believe the monastery to be the easy answer to their neediness. They certainly weren't quick to allow anyone to depend on them. "Easy admission is not to be granted," Benedict advises, which seems to be putting it mildly. And then he quotes from 1 John 4:1, "Beloved, do not believe every spirit, but test the spirits to see whether they are from God."

"After four of five days" Benedict says, if he has had the patience to persist that long, and only then, you should allow the man to come in and stay as a guest for a while.[6] Even then, if the man says that he has come with the intention of becoming a monk, the older monks are to continue to test his resolve and spirit. "All the things that are hard and repugnant to nature in the way to God are to be expounded to him." Two months after his arrival, he is supposed to sit and listen to Benedict's complete Rule read out for him.

Then, the monks were to ask him if he was willing to live by its precepts. If still unbowed, the man would finally be shown the novices' quarters, "and once again his patience under all kinds of trials is to be put to the test." There was no let-up on a man who thought that monastic life was his calling.

Over the course of the next twelve months, after many more tests, and at least two more readings of the complete Rule, a novice would be permitted to join the community. He was to be told in no uncertain terms that he may never "cast off from his neck the yoke of the Rule," and "must promise in the oratory, in the presence of all, stability, conversion of life and obedience."

"Given all of that, what's the spirituality of dependence?" I asked Luke.

"We still test a novice like you wouldn't believe!" Luke explained. "Nine years, it usually takes, living here under the Rule and in obedience before you may make your solemn vows." *Nine years!*

"It only works," he iterated, "because we are utterly and completely dependent on each other. Not just on God, but on each other. You have probably been taught to believe that you have to stand on your own two feet, that sort of thing. We all have been taught that. The American Way, right? But there's an alternative; it's Christ's alternative—a spirituality of dependence."

———⟡———

"God Alone" are the words in large block letters cut in stone above your head as you enter the Abbey of Gethsemani in Kentucky. I can't imagine that such a slogan would ever be used by Madison Avenue to sell a product or service, but it certainly focuses my attention. And once you enter inside, the setting is as simply austere as the outside may be extravagantly beautiful.

"Yes, you and God—alone together—have got to find your unique way of getting along—but that doesn't mean you are getting along on your own. You're supposed to need other people," Luke says to me one day.

"There's nothing wrong with being needy, but it's best to understand your needs rather than be fooled by them. For instance, if you walk into your home church drunk next week, it's almost certain that people will notice. But if you walk into church in unbelief instead, but faking it and going through the motions of the service as if nothing is wrong, you'll get along just fine. You'll likely fool everyone.

"According to what Jesus had to say in the gospels, you'd be better off drunk. Still, we assume that our unbelief is not a problem. We can fake it.

"I'm not suggesting that unbelief is like a disease to be cured, or even that it's unusual, or limiting. Doubt and unbelief are flipsides to faith. In fact, in a deeply vowed life, spiritual and intellectual doubt make sense. It's not even something to be confessed. It's not wrong," Luke said.

Dean Koontz writes in his horror novel, *Brother Odd*, "Living in a monastery, even as a guest rather than as a monk, you have more opportunities than you might have elsewhere to see the world as it is, instead of through the shadow that you cast upon it."[7] So true, because few men in the monastery care a wit about what sort of shadow they in fact cast. Perhaps that is why the monks seem to see through me and have taught me to acknowledge my intellectual faith troubles, my lazy practices, my unreal talk, my patterns of avoiding God.

Father Luke and other monks have taught me to examine a lot of things that I'm usually good at masking.

3

BECOMING REAL

everything
"move right fist several times from left to right quickly at
just below chest level but slightly to side of body"
—*A Dictionary of the Cistercian Sign Language*

I've often wondered, after returning home with the glow
of retreat still on my face, *Why don't I live at home
more closely to what I love at a monastery? Surely it
wouldn't be too difficult to make some changes in order to
do that?* Monastic practices can be duplicated elsewhere,
even in the loudest, busiest, and most urban of settings.
But without brothers doing likewise, my spirit fades after
a while.

I have learned that it can be subconsciously frustrating
to be judged on an entirely new and different set of criteria.

Why don't they seem more happy to see me? I found myself wondering one day.

I once asked Father Luke if there was any hope for me in the contemplative life, since prayer seems to come so hard for me. I explained that the harder I try to pray while cutting the grass, doing the dishes, or just sitting still, the harder it seems to remain on task.

"In any kind of prayer the first ten or fifteen minutes—okay, Jon, for you perhaps longer!" here Luke laughed out loud, "is going to be about what's on your mind. 'I have to make that phone call. I have to go and get that thing.' And so on.

"You cannot come to any union with God until those things work themselves out of you. But," and he paused, "be patient. You have time. A moment of union, just a moment, is all that you need."

"A moment of union is all that you need." What a revelation that was! Luke gave me hope that what I was doing actually had some benefit. *I have some good moments. They are brief, but a moment is, by definition, brief.* John of the Cross wrote, "An instant of pure love is more precious in the eyes of God and the soul . . . than all other good works together, though it may seem as if nothing were done."[1]

I had driven on a Friday afternoon from Nashville over the mountains through Chattanooga and down into Atlanta, on my way to a long weekend twenty miles west of Atlanta, at Our Lady of the Holy Spirit in Conyers, Georgia. Since it was a Friday afternoon, the traffic was heavy, and driving through Atlanta while anticipating the respite of the abbey, I became very tense. In the first batch of traffic around the beltway, I began honking my horn at the more relaxed commuters.

"What are they doing!" I began yelling to my windshield. "Get moving!"

If you've ever driven through Atlanta at rush hour, you know what happens. The traffic never let up until I was well past the city and just about to reach my Conyers exit off of Route 20. I realized, as I drove through the abbey front gate, that I was still traveling at about twice the posted legal speed, and had screamed at someone from my car only moments beforehand.

When I finally arrived and Father Ambrose met me at the retreat house front desk, he looked very matter of fact.

"Hello, Jon. Welcome," he said.

"It's really good to be here," I exhaled.

For many people, *the monastery* is the only place where faith and spirituality remain pristine, untouched by doctrinal battles, untainted by scandals. The monks' lack of touch with the world has kept them outside the fray of many of the intra-church fights and scandals that periodically beset denominations. In fact, the monastery is set apart in some meaningful ways, for good or for ill. Monasteries are almost entirely set apart from church politics. They play no formal role in the life of the diocese where they reside. Each monastery's abbot reports to a regional director of sorts, and then to the pope. Monasteries are in many ways like religious islands.

I love monasteries because the people in them and the people who visit them tend to look at life in essential terms. In my local church—and believe me, I love my church—we've mostly stopped asking questions that someone seems to have decided a while ago were no longer practical. Questions such as: Is evil real, or do people simply act that way from time to time? What is heaven? What is good? Instead, we're very practical in my church. We *do* things. But sometimes I miss the essential.

Thomas Merton once said, "A monk is a man who has been called by the Holy Spirit to relinquish the cares, desires and ambitions of other men, and devote his entire life to seeking God. The concept is familiar. The reality which the concept signifies is a mystery."[2] In my experience, monks seem to feel that way: their lives are a mystery even to themselves. Not that they don't know what to do—it's very clear what a Trappist monk does from season to season, day to day, hour to hour—but they are never entirely sure, or they're always a bit dissatisfied, with their understanding of who they are. So am I.

"There is more to me underneath what you see," Father Ambrose said to me on that Georgia afternoon, well after I had forgotten the irritating traffic outside. And that of course made perfect sense. *I hope that the same is true of me.*

Then he added: "There is a no-name me that only God knows. When I am alone with God, it is that no-name me, that me without masks and with a true identity, known only by him, that listens. Someday, perhaps only in eternity, I will know who the real me is."

⸙

"The work of becoming real with God takes a lifetime," Father Ambrose repeated the next morning. It was a noisy morning by monastic standards, as workers were reinforcing a cement wall on the church just outside our window. We huddled closely together as we talked so as to hear each other clearly. After a short while we gave up. "It's time for lunch, anyway," Ambrose said.

When we arrived at the refectory, the blessing had already been pronounced and monks and retreatants were lined up to serve themselves soup, salad, and fresh bread. It is common to sit away from friends at mealtime in the monastery, and so Ambrose went to a different table from mine.

The pea soup was delicious, and I began questioning the old monk sitting across from me about how many years he had spent in the Georgia abbey.

"Thirty-five," he said.

"Wow, that's a long time."

"Not really," Francis replied matter-of-factly. "I'm one of the youngest men here." Francis was well into his seventies, not a young man by any measure; he had gone to college and had a career for more than a decade before knocking on the abbey door for the first time. He thought himself a "young monk" after more than thirty-five years.

I thought he was putting me on. *This is a monk joke,* I thought. *Maybe they lie in these small, playful ways because the bigger, more adventurous sins are really out of bounds. Let's have some fun with the young retreatant still in shirtsleeves.*

"No, I'm quite serious," Francis said. And he pulled a piece of paper from his pocket, grabbed the pen from mine, and began to write, counting all of the men who live in the monastery out loud to himself:

Entered before '69	25 men
Francis '69	1
After Francis	14
	That's 40 professed men.
Plus, the non-professed	9
Total here	49 men

Sure enough, he was one of the youngest monks there after thirty-five years.

———∞∞∞———

Reading in the Refectory

Visit almost any Cistercian or Benedictine monastery at mealtime and you'll be treated to an ancient tradition, when a designated monk reads while the others eat. In the refectory the reading is done by one of the brothers, while everyone else eats in silence. St. Benedict's Rule—which is certainly no longer followed to the letter on many matters—puts it this way: "There is to be complete silence, so that no whisper nor any voice other than that of the reader be heard there. Whatever is wanted for eating and drinking the brethren should pass to one another, so that no one need ask for anything. If, however, something is wanted, it should be asked for by some sign or sound rather than by speaking."[3] Sometimes this takes place throughout the meal, other times only for part of the time. In European abbeys, the reading brother will be perched above, in a space that looks like a pulpit, or as one writer puts it, "like a martin's nest."[4] The books are usually selected by the abbot, and they are not necessarily spiritual. I once spent two lunches at a priory in Vermont listening to a new history of the Civil War.

A small library sits in each Trappist retreat house, filled with the products of the labors of M. Basil Pennington and other monks who feverishly translated and produced the writings of the Cistercian Fathers over the last thirty-plus years. Dom Basil founded Cistercian Publications in the 1970s, and since then they have published English translations of Cistercian classics, treatises on brotherly love, spiritual commentaries and homilies on books of the Bible such as the Song of Songs, commentaries on the Rule of St. Benedict, and many other odd and interesting things you'll find in the small retreat house library.

Of all the books that one might find in a library, any library, it is Margery Williams's children's book, *The Velveteen Rabbit*, that has stuck with me. That doesn't mean I understood its lessons when I first read it at the age of four or five. No, it made sense to me when Father Ambrose told me to read it again while on retreat in my mid-thirties.

I'll take the teaching of the Skin Horse over something in Thomas Aquinas any day. *The Velveteen Rabbit* begins like this—do you remember? "There was once a velveteen rabbit, and in the beginning he was really splendid. He was fat and bunchy, as a rabbit should be; his coat was spotted brown and white, he had real thread whiskers, and his ears were lined with pink sateen."

And then the shiny new velveteen rabbit meets the other toys in the nursery. "The Skin Horse had lived longer in the nursery than any of the others. He was so old that his brown coat was bald in patches and showed the seams underneath, and most of the hairs in his tail had been pulled out to string bead necklaces. He was wise, for he had seen a long succession of mechanical toys arrive to boast and swagger, and by-and-by break their mainsprings and pass away, and he knew that they were only toys, and would never turn into anything else. For nursery magic is very strange and wonderful, and only those playthings that are old and wise and experienced like the Skin Horse understand all about it."

"What is REAL?" asked the Rabbit one day, when they were lying side by side near the nursery fender, before Nana came to tidy the room. "Does it mean having things that buzz inside you and a stick-out handle?"

"Real isn't how you are made," said the Skin Horse. "It's a thing that happens to you. When a child loves you for a long, long time, not just to play with, but REALLY loves you, then you become Real."

"Does it hurt?" asked the Rabbit.

"Sometimes," said the Skin Horse, for he was always truthful. "When you are Real you don't mind being hurt."

"Does it happen all at once, like being wound up," he asked, "or bit by bit?"

"It doesn't happen all at once," said the Skin Horse. "You become. It takes a long time. That's why it doesn't happen often to people who break easily, or have sharp edges, or who have to be carefully kept. Generally, by the time you are Real, most of your hair has been loved off, and your eyes drop out and you get loose in the joints and very shabby. But these things don't matter at all, because once you are Real you can't be ugly, except to people who don't understand."

"I suppose *you* are real?" said the Rabbit. And then he wished he had not said it, for he thought the Skin Horse might be sensitive. But the Skin Horse only smiled.

"The Boy's Uncle made me Real," he said. "That was a great many years ago; but once you are Real you can't become unreal again. It lasts for always."[5]

I saw Father Ambrose a few months later, on another retreat, and reminded him that he had recommended *The Velveteen Rabbit*. "Is an old monk like the Skin Horse?" I asked him mischievously.

"God willing!" he replied.

My monk friends tell me that becoming real is what the process of *conversion* is all about. Conversion means some very specific things in a monastic context—things that make good sense for non-monastics as well.

Etymologically, conversion means "changed" or perhaps "improved." It comes from the Latin word *conversus*, which is intended to be the opposite of *nutritus* or "nursed." Nursed were those boys promised by their parents to the monastery as infants. They were figuratively "nursed" by the monastic life, growing up in their schools. This designation might be akin to how we speak of "cradle Presbyterians," etc., today—those who have never meaningfully stepped outside of the belief and practice of their tradition. The *nutriti* were, however, highly regarded in the medieval monasteries. Until the

52

time of the Cistercian reforms of the eleventh and twelfth centuries—when they asked that only adults come—it was from the ranks of the *nutriti* that all of their leaders arose.

In contrast, the *conversi* or converts were those who had come later in life, usually without the benefit of formal education, and they almost always remained lay, or non-priestly, brothers. It was these men who did most of the physical work of the monastery, while the *nutriti* chanted in the choir, sung the Mass, and spent hours in spiritual reading and prayer.

But for Saint Benedict and many of his followers, *conversus* took on a different meaning. They taught monks—and any man who sought to be like one—the importance of a "conversion of life." All of Benedict's monks were supposed to take seriously the continual reformation necessary in their lives, to continually convert, so that Christ may be more and more present in their lives.

This is the understanding of conversion that predominates in monastic spirituality today. Conversion does not happen in a moment; it happens over the course of a lifetime. Even then, a lifetime extends beyond our earthly existence and so it is more like an eternity. "Be patient," monks have told me over and over again. "What's your rush?"

"It doesn't happen all at once," said the Skin Horse. "You become. It takes a long time."

I used to resent this advice, thinking that they simply did not understand what real life was like. *It's easy to say that you are all about conversion when you have so much time available to think about it!*

Nearly twenty years ago I was mostly happily married and living in a dive of an apartment on the North Shore of Boston. It was 1991, and by this time in my life I actually had a few

Catholic friends and had joined a Thomas Merton Society chapter in Boston.

I made my first visit to St. Joseph's Abbey back then, together with my Merton group. Inside the little retreat house that sits along the state highway, the furnishings remind me of the sort of things that once sat in my grandparents' summer cottage by a lake in Michigan. Knitted doilies on the end-tables, a row of country living magazines lie accordion-style on a long coffee table, sturdy handmade chairs of wood. There's a tiny makeshift kitchen in the corner with a large tin teapot and a loaf of bread that makes me wonder what enormous pan it must have burst out of.

Dom Basil Pennington walks in, having strolled down the long driveway from the monastery on the hill above. All I notice at first are his feet. *They are enormous*, I thought to myself. He's wearing sandals that show his toe-knuckles and leg-hair, but it's the size of the feet that astonishes. He's called *Dom*, the Latin for *Father*, and it seems to fit him well. With physical characteristics that mirror his spirit, Dom Basil really is out of this world, not a typical priest.

Does he know that he looks like an enormous Jesus? I wonder to myself, as we're all sitting down.

"If God is everywhere, then why do we go looking for him?" Father Basil said to our group of retreatants seeking wisdom in the ways of centering prayer. We all sat in a circle and it felt a little embarrassing, facing each other.

Each of us in our little group was a wanderer of one sort or another. Basil knew his audience well; or, was it that he simply knew the human spirit? Bill, one of the oldest members of our group, was aging and balding and lived alone in downtown Boston. He taught Latin in a secondary school, but he'd done it forever and always felt that there was something he was missing in life. Judith and Ken met each other while in France during their junior year of college and had moved around the U.S. several times in the last ten years taking different jobs in different cities.

I thought of myself as a wanderer back then, a spiritual explorer of sorts, who had grown restless or dissatisfied in one denomination and then moved on to another, from one church to another. Friends of mine had even started their own churches. More than apple pie and baseball, a self-constructed religion is probably the real American Way. If you aren't satisfied with who you are, change yourself, recreate yourself, and do the same with your religion. In most areas of life, we want to know what's new. What's new is always more interesting than what's old.

Ever since the Renaissance when philosopher Francis Bacon popularized the scientific method of inquiry, faith in progress or what's new has eaten away at Christian faith. Christians have lost hope and the world has lost hope in Christian faith. But hanging out with monks cannot help but reverse this trend a bit. Monastics have deepened in me an appreciation for what is old rather than what is new. They have taught me to seek what is true and ancient; to go deeper, rather than to go seeking something else.

"Where can God be found, if God is all around us?" Dom Basil asked us. "Where do we go to listen for his voice?" They were rhetorical questions—I knew that much—but I didn't know the answers. "Do you know who you really are? How can you find that out?"

St. Joseph's Abbey has a mission statement that reads, "Cistercian monks are known traditionally as lovers of the brethren and the place. The community of Spencer sees itself as an expression of the mystery of the Church, where nothing is preferred to the love of Christ in praise of the Father's glory . . . By fidelity to our monastic way of life, which has its own hidden mode of apostolic fruitfulness, we perform a service for God's people and the whole human race."

"I do believe it," Father Luke once said to me, after I read him that paragraph, a decade after that first encounter with Dom Basil. "There is value to silence and this sort of life for the world-at-large that the world-at-large doesn't usually comprehend. We help people who come here to be more real in their lives, to uncover some reality. And the hidden mode we speak of is what the spirit and prayer of the monks accomplish for the Church and the world that can never really be measured. That's okay," he concluded with a grin, "immeasurable results."

Even an activist Christian like Desmond Tutu understands this "hidden mode of apostolic fruitfulness." Tutu once explained the value of monasticism by retelling the gospel story of a paralytic whom Jesus healed. After being lowered down through a hole in the roof by his friends, "we are told that when our Lord saw their faith, i.e. the faith of the friends, then he said to the paralytic, 'Your sins are forgiven.'" Tutu concludes: "This principle of vicariousness I have thought applies so aptly to [monks and nuns] . . . I believe that all [of them] have this peculiar vicarious ministry, being there on behalf of, for the sake of, others."[6]

Monks don't build programs. There are no "program" monasteries like there are program churches. Occasionally, you will find a monastery that titles or gives themes to its weekend or week-long retreats—this has recently begun to happen—but this is not the usual custom. An abbey is built on ancient premises, lost in most parts of Christianity, of the older instructing the younger. All are welcome, but you cannot be quite sure of what you will experience before experiencing it. Mentors, spiritual directors, and wise men all make sense in a monastery, but programs don't.

There's no curriculum or course of study for becoming a contemplative. If it were programmatic there would be no, or certainly fewer, books about it. All that you need is life-experience, God's grace, a teacher or two, and time spent— which is all easier written than done. Paul said, "Work out your own salvation with fear and trembling; for it is God who is at work in you" (Phil. 2:12–13). Paul couldn't create a direct relationship between the Almighty and each individual member of his congregations—they had to work at doing that all by themselves.

The contemplative way of life is available to every person on the planet—even the monks tell me that. I certainly don't have it, not yet, but I'm working it out.

Just as monks don't really have programs, they also don't make many promises, and it's frustrating.

"We can show you how to be quiet, how to listen, but only God can show you the other stuff," Father Ambrose told me long ago.

"What stuff?"

"You."

4

FRIENDSHIP AND MEANING

to give
"push forward open right hand with palm up and fingers
held together tightly"

—*A Dictionary of the Cistercian Sign Language*

I was supposed to drive down and meet Father Luke at the
retreat house by 2 p.m. "Don't come, Jon," he e-mailed
me early on a January morning. "Many of us have colds,
including me, and some of them are now turning into pneumonia. We're all sick!"

This was deeply disappointing, as I was badly wanting to
speak with Luke. I was having a rough week in the middle
of a rough year. After nearly twenty years of marriage, my
wife, my college sweetheart, was thinking about separation
and divorce. It hadn't exactly taken me by surprise; we had
already endured a few years of tough times, but she was
thinking of giving up on our marriage and I was shaken to
the core. I *needed* to talk with Father Luke on this day.

I've learned that getting in touch with a monk in a hurry rarely works out. Deceleration is their way of life.

It was actually four days later when Father Luke and I finally settled down in comfortable chairs in the retreat house library. This is the room where monks meet and counsel with retreatants. It is also where they will often greet their family and friends who have traveled from far away to spend a day with their brother, son, or friend.

Luke looks tired today, I thought to myself. *Do I look that tired? I certainly feel how he looks.* His white hair seemed more ruffled than usual, and he was sitting heavier in his chair. Usually Luke sits lightly, like someone who enjoys jumping up to greet someone new or to fetch a book from a shelf. *Remember, of course, that he's older than your father.*

"Are you feeling all right today?" I ask.

"Oh yes, Jon, thank you for asking. I'm just not sleeping very well. Still getting over that little bout with pneumonia, you know? I'm not just getting older—I've been saying that for too long—I *am* old," he said with a broad smile.

One of the best things about coming to see Father Luke is seeing his smile.

He continued, "Since many of the brothers are in the infirmary just now with bad colds and some flu, I have been staying up with them from time to time. We sit with each other, you know."

Monastic life is hard, to be sure, but it can't be as hard as living alone without good friends.

"Tell me about intimacy, the intimacy of friendship, please," I said, almost imploringly. What I didn't say was, *I'm losing my wife and it's killing me. I need to hear how it is supposed to work. Why is my most intimate relationship fading away before my eyes?*

"What is intimacy between friends—as you live it in the monastery?" I said, detaching myself from the emotions.

Luke paused for a minute and looked out the window searching for his words.

"All love is a gift, Jon. Why should anyone love me?

"The kind of intimate friendship and love that monks have for each other—or that anyone, I imagine, has for another—is completely unnatural, I think," he said.

"Really?" I was surprised.

"Yes, don't you think so?"

"I hadn't thought of it that way before," I said.

"Monks, at least, are too competitive to naturally love each other. Somehow, in some way, God shows us the beauty of another man's soul, and that's the beginning of true love. It's grace," Luke explained.

"But you work at it too, right?" I asked.

"Yes, that's true. The goal of the monastic life is so narrowed to self-giving that you almost can't help but love. But its beginning and sustaining energy are purely unnatural."

"Love as a gift—I really haven't thought of it that way," I told him. "I find myself trying harder and harder to love, or to fix the situations in my life when love seems to be fleeting or absent."

Luke looked at me sincerely. "It's true that when you see a guy doing something pure and unheralded at 3:15 a.m., it's hard not to realize that he must be a good guy. It is easier to love him, then."

"What about when one of the guys drives you nuts, what do you do, then?"

"Well, that's always interesting," he began. And then Luke described what it is like to take this sort of problem to his abbot. "You'll tell the Abbot that so-and-so is being difficult or impossible, or that you simply cannot get along with him, and the Abbot will say something like, 'Well how long has he been doing this?' 'Thirty or forty years,' I'll say. 'So, you think that he's going to change now?' The message is clear—and I've learned it by now: *you* are the one who needs to change."

———— ❦ ————

Most experts say that we live in a time of more dramatic change than any other in history. I am able, today, to sit online at the feet of some of the greatest contemplative teachers of the last century. There are YouTube videos of Bede Griffiths and Thomas Keating, as well as lectures of Merton and Wayne Teasdale and many others. I have spent hours with these videos. Just as I have no great desire to be in the stands at the Super Bowl because I can see the game best from my seat at home, I am now able to get closer to much of what I need than I ever could have, before.

But human relationships communicate wisdom better than can ever happen through a secondary medium. Perhaps Christians have explored Eastern religions because of this special feature: you spend time face-to-face with your guru and he challenges you in specific ways. The face-to-face teaching startles you into catching on a whole lot quicker. Just like in Zen, Christian faith is supposed to be a way of life more than a system of doctrines, and learning how to live the life only happens in one-on-one training.

It's physical; it's presence. The existence of monks, even today, is evidence of faith that is anti-Gnostic; it is about what you do with your life, your body, and your passions—not just your brain.

———— ❦ ————

The first five centuries of Christianity were basically episcopal. In other words, Christianity was governed by bishops and

A Monk's Daily Routine

A decade before the Second Vatican Council (1962–65), the British travel-writer Michael Leigh Fermor wrote the following:

> A Trappist monk rises at one or two in the morning according to the season. Seven hours of his day are spent in church, singing the offices, kneeling or standing in silent meditation, often in the dark. The remainder of the day passes in field-labour of the most primitive and exhausting kind; in mental prayer and in sermons and readings from the Martyrology. Leisure and recreation are unheard of, and, in practice if not in theory, very little time is devoted to study . . . At every season the monks are compelled to wear the same heavy clothing, a regulation almost unbearable in the rustic toils of midsummer . . . There are no cells. All, from the Abbot downwards, sleep in cubicles in a dormitory on palliasses of straw stretched out on bare planks. Heating does not exist and the monks lie down to sleep in their habits with their hoods pulled over their heads.[1]

If you've read *The Seven Storey Mountain* you've encountered similar descriptions. As a young monk in Kentucky in the 1940s, Merton chronicled all of these things with aplomb and complaint. But today, Trappist monks no longer:

- rise at 1 or 2 a.m.—they rise in time for Vigils at 4 a.m.,
- do much by way of manual labor—their work is less strenuous,
- wear heavy clothing out of season,
- sleep in a common area—they have small, private rooms called cells,
- sleep in their formal religious clothing,
- do without heat in winter or without air-conditioning in summer. At least infirmaries, libraries, and some offices will have cooling units running in the summer months.

The era is also gone when Benedictine monks of all kinds distinguished between "choir" monks and "lay brothers." This former class system was a way of separating the educated ones from the uneducated. Today, all monks do basically the same things, whether physical work or singing in choir. Each has his gifts and talents, but no one is immune from any sort of activity.

clergy, and then eventually, by the bishop of Rome, who became known as the pope. Early Christians established doctrine and ceremony and sacrament. Then, for the next thousand years, the faith became more dispersed, disorganized, unruly—or at least it did in relation to its original episcopal organization. At the same time, monasteries became a draw for some of the faithful because they were places where the faith was not only preserved but nurtured in one-on-one transmission of practice and understanding. Man-to-man and woman-to-woman, and then on rare occasions there were coed experiments (the earliest Franciscans, some of the Beguine communities in France), but these situations didn't last for long.

Like Zen masters, Christian abbots, priors and prioresses, anchorites and hermits, mentored individual men and women in the ways of following Christ. They became living tutorials in ways that could not have happened if teaching had only been taking place in church. So it is with my visits to see monks.

I've always been drawn to elders. My grandparents were influential when I was young and I idolized my two grandfathers. In college, I quickly became a teacher's assistant not only for the extra cash, but for the relationships with professors. In seminary I latched on to a couple of professors in particular, gleaning all that I could from them in office chats and over lunches. Even today, I am a member of a book group that meets on Wednesday mornings and consists of the rector of our church, five women who range in age from sixty-four to ninety, and me. I love it.

So when I get on the Web to listen and watch great teachers, it can only take me so far. Father Luke, and others like him, offer something tangible to me. I feel like my camel is wandering around outside in the grass while I'm listening to one of the Desert Fathers.

———— ∞ ————

That same afternoon when we talked about intimacy, I asked Father Luke about stability.

"Tell me about your vow of stability. What I mean is, have you ever doubted it? No, wait: that is not really a fair question—don't answer that. What I mean is, what happens when a brother wants to break his vow?"

Luke thought deeply. *Is he remembering someone in particular?* I wondered. I was. I was thinking of my situation at home.

"It happens so rarely," he replied, after a short while.

"But when it does happen, how is it interpreted? Does a brother breaking his vow mean that somehow that vow was wrong from the beginning?" I was still struggling to understand my own troubles, and asking him about it without asking him about it.

"No, I don't think so. I suppose that occasionally it might be thought that he had been immature when he originally joined; but no, I don't think so.

"We spend around nine years in community before solemn vows! That's a long time—intended to make it clear to all that we know what we're doing," he said, but clearly this wasn't Father Luke's favorite subject.

"Well, then, if a brother leaves, is it ever treated like an annulment in a marriage?" I asked.

"Yes, I suppose that it is. To leave the monastery by being released from your vow can be like annulment in that the sacrament no longer exists. In fact, it's the reverse: what was once a sacrament, a means of grace, has become the opposite. The life you had vowed to live has ceased to be nourishing."

On another rainy afternoon I told Father Luke about how I had come close to choosing the monastic life back when I was twenty. Looking out our windows, sheets of water were falling across the hillside and the gutters were roaring with the sound of it. He surprised me by responding, "You can't say that you *choose* a monastic life. No one can. It is so unnatural a way of life that no one would or could choose it for themselves," he said.

"*I* would," I told him earnestly.

"No you wouldn't. You can't do it without grace. You, like all of us, would be fidgeting around and calculating your next visit to Rome. Without grace, you are not at rest in this or any other sort of life.

"It must begin with God. As Saint Bernard of Clairvaux put it, 'His desire gives rise to yours,'" Luke said.

A man is never supposed to enter the monastery in order to avoid facing some personal problems in his life. Monks are adept at discerning what we're avoiding.

One of my monastic friends once told me of profound feelings he had for a young woman in his early twenties, before he entered the monastery. Accepting a call to monastic life was, for him, a matter of surrendering joyfully to another possession, or claim, on his life and being unable to deny its priority, "even though the other, erotic, love was still quivering painfully," he explained in a letter.

"There's no sense denying that you feel something," he wrote to me. "It's what you do with your feelings that matters."

It also used to be the case, a half-century or longer ago, that young men were prepared for the monastery in the same way that they were prepared to become British Members of Parliament, or to attend a fine university. The monastery was just one more vocation a young man might take for himself, or be given. There was nothing particularly remarkable about it. And it was a short distance from being at home with a governess to singing Latin chant in the monastery choir.

This is no longer so, obviously. Only adults are welcome to the monastery; it is supposed to be a mature decision. And you will try in vain to find a mother or father who earnestly desires for their son to enter the cloister.

Father Bernard is the kind of man you wish you knew. He's the sort of guy that novels are written about: full of quirks and small faults, but gracious, good, and earnest. Christians rarely use the Yiddish word *mensch*, but that's what Bernard is. He's a good person, which is not to say he is holy. That's the difference between a mensch and a saint: a mensch has no pretence to special holiness; instead, he or she possesses an essential and abundant *humanness*. Graham Greene puts it best in one of his novels when he writes how it is better to have a "cracked character where the truth might occasionally seed" than to be "like a wall so plastered over with church announcements that you couldn't even see the patchwork behind."[2]

At about eighty years old, Bernard looks like he's in his sixties. He walks confidently, wearing blue jeans while he's working in the fields and stables around his monastery. He talks with a quiet confidence. If he didn't wear a monk's cowl from time to time, he could be a Los Angeles detective in a pulp fiction novel from the 1940s. He's a bit of a wise guy, always with a joke at his own expense.

Bernard also loves to learn and is hesitant to teach. When I ask him a question, he tells me a story from his own life. When I come back again and again to hear the funny stories he has to tell, he seems surprised that I would be so interested as to sit and listen. Bernard has learned far more outside of classrooms, during a life of experience and reflection, than inside of them.

He remembers the day he first hoofed it all the way to the monastery as if it was last week. It was actually a July afternoon in 1936, and he was 17. Bernard told his parents that he was walking the seven miles to the monastery for Mass; he didn't mention that he had a letter in his pocket from his pastor and confessor recommending him as an ideal monastic candidate.

"We all keep little secrets, don't we?" he winks at me.

The vocation director at the abbey met with Bernard and read the letter from his priest, "adjusting his pince-nez, sitting pinched on the bridge of his old French nose," as Bernard remembers it. The Order of Cistercians originated in 1098 at Citeaux Abbey, in France, and the leaders of the American abbeys were still usually French in the first half of the twentieth century.

"He read out loud: 'Four years of Latin, three years of Greek, ten years of French.'" Bernard was well educated, as most Catholic schoolboys once were, and his priest had laid out his credentials in the letter.

" 'When can you join us?' the vocation director asked, looking up at me. Those were simpler days in many ways," Bernard explained.

And so Bernard walked the seven miles back home and told his parents the truth. His mother wept—"tears and lamentations," Bernard described—but on the following day he returned to the monastery with his things. One month later his parents came to the abbey, realizing that their son didn't seem to be coming home, and tried to force him to return. Parents have done this sort of thing for centuries. The relatives of St. Clare of Assisi tried to literally drag her away.

"We'll call the police!" his father said.

"Go ahead," Bernard replied, or at least that's how he remembers having replied 75 years later.

His mother was wiser. Unhappy to have lost her son, she nevertheless left him another suitcase of starched shirts. And she tucked fudge underneath, at the bottom. A few years later, at the service of his solemn profession (final vows), Bernard's mother brought sandwiches for all of the invited guests.

Father Ambrose is another one like Brother Bernard. You get the feeling that Father Ambrose is a man who has always

Latin Spiritual Phrases

Although Cistercian monks no longer talk in Latin to one another in the abbey, they still use the language in their daily liturgy, and in certain special phrases having to do with the spiritual life. Most of all is *pax*, "peace." And the description of their life from the Rule, *ora et labora*, "pray and work." *Puritas cordis*—"purity of heart" and *in veritate*—"in truth" are two others. One of my favorites, which I try to keep on my lips at difficult times, is *humilitas mentis*, "lowliness of mind." And then it is traditional, when a novice master is teaching his students, for the teacher to conclude each session by saying, *Benedicite*. And the men respond, *Dominus*. "Bless you." And, "Lord." Finally, consider *ut in omnibus glorificetur Deus*, "that in everything may God be glorified" (Rule, ch. 57.9).

had his act together. He is kind and loving, but a monk's love can be surprisingly adult, without sentimentality. It has a depth and warmth for friends and strangers both, but also a real honesty. The friendship of monks—mostly with each other, not necessarily with me—seems more intimate to me than the average marriage.

Father Ambrose once described his life to me by saying, "I entered the world of planet Earth, USA, Oklahoma City, around midnight on September 1, 1924. I entered the world of monasticism at about 3 p.m., September 6, 1947. When I arrived at the monastery I had only 23 years worth of human experience and a myriad of questions."

Ambrose loved a woman before entering the monastery, and we have been able to talk about it. He told me, "In the end, I could not surrender joyfully to the possession of that love because another claim on my life had been thrust before me, and my heart could not deny its priority. So I entered monastic life with a bagful of experiences. And in a culture of silence dedicated to conversing with God and reflective awareness, I kept hearing about love as the real business of life. With age and experience, I've come to understand it much more."

Then his mind turned to the love that he embraced most of all, his love for God. As he described it, tears welled up in the corners of his eyelids. "Please forgive me," he said. Ambrose *feels* his words in a way that I rarely do. "I sometimes weep at what seem to be the oddest times. It's embarrassing, even for an old fart like me," he said. To this day, I don't think I have witnessed again a man in tears who had not a trace of shame.

Friendship is complicated, and monks are no exception. Monks are so independent and dependent all at the same time.

I've seen arguments, both verbal and passive, in monasteries. Monastics are very human.

"There's nothing wrong with disagreements," Ambrose said to me one day. "I argue with the Abbot from time to time. But we love each other."

"We argue, but we are close. We are hermits in community," Father Luke said during one of our early afternoon sessions in the retreat house. "Just as you can be alone in your relationship with God, we deliberately spend many hours alone, especially on feast days and holidays."

"Do you get lonely?" I asked him.

"I'm not sure if I'd ever call it that," he said, sitting up straighter in his wooden chair. "But you have to learn how to use your time well. You don't exactly recreate. But you read, walk, garden. There's plenty of time, but you have to fill your time with good things."

Trappists live most of their days in silence—a practice that can be traced back to the habits of the first men who walked into the deserts outside of the cities of the Roman Empire. The very first rules for monastic life praised silence, and monks have always quoted James 1:26 in this regard: "If any [one] think they are religious, and do not bridle their tongues but deceive their hearts, their religion is worthless." St. Benedict also quoted Proverbs 10:19 in chapter six of his Rule, which is devoted to the subject of silence: "When words are many, transgression is not lacking, but the prudent are restrained in speech."

Laurence Freeman recently said, "The work of silence creates community," and our too-noisy lives are a primary reason for our lack of feeling and being together.[3] However, there are challenges to friendship in these sorts of circumstances. In *The Heart of the Matter*, Graham Greene wrote about the darkness and intimacy of living in close community: "Here you could love human beings nearly as God loved them, knowing the worst."[4] This must be true of living in a cloister. There is no escaping the bad qualities of the brother whose cell is next to yours, or the brother whose personal habits rub you the wrong way at Compline each evening. Most of us only know the members of our families in these close ways.

Basil Pennington used to explain that being a contemplative is like being a lover. I'm quite sure that Basil never knew the experience of a physical lover, but he talked as if he did because his relationship with God was modeled on it. A Trappist monk is a lover in the way of the Song of Songs. They take much of their spirituality from the Song; their great founder, St. Bernard of Clairvaux, preached eighty-six sermons on it, interpreting the erotic bits in allegorical ways. Like Bernard before him, Basil knew "spiritual" marriage of a mystic sort.

And Basil would tell me, "If you want to understand the contemplative life, think about what it was like when you first met the most important love affair of your life. How did it begin, and get nurtured?

"Did you ask questions? Did you want to know things about her? What did you do in those early days? You just enjoyed her presence, didn't you? And then, sometimes, you came to a point where talking seemed almost unnecessary."

If the way to God is a straight line—and we all know that it is not—then there is a place on that line where communion begins to turn into union. This isn't mystical fancy, but just the way it is. And then, an intimate friendship with God feeds every other relationship we have. "In fact, the two seem to feed each other, back and forth," Father Luke once explained as we sat in our paneled room in the retreat house. How I have grown to love that room!

"Love of God and neighbor—that's it, right? Well, the second won't happen very well without the first. And your neighbor, your brother, your partner, even when he infuriates you, shows you something about yourself and about God that you cannot ignore," Luke said that day.

Thomas Merton once wrote, "When you meet an interesting stranger you find yourself alert and curious . . . You seek to discover something of the mystery of his identity and of his history. At the same time if he inspires confidence, if he seems to be a person of unusual depth and experience, you begin to open up to him and to share with him the secret of your own life. In this way, a true personal encounter brings us not only knowledge of another, fellow-

Silence and Scripture Reading

Just as most lectionary cycles avoid the more militaristic Psalms, so too did St. Benedict encourage certain portions of the Bible be read more than others. In chapter 42 of his Rule, Benedict instructs monks to keep silence during the night. After Compline (late in the evening), all are to be completely silent. But even prior to that, when darkness settles in, he asked the monks to sit together and for one of them to read aloud to the others. He advised that they read works such as the *Conferences* of John Cassian, or the Lives of the Fathers, both accounts of the lives and practices of previous monks and saints. He adds, "Or some other work which will edify the hearers, but not the Heptateuch [an old term for the first seven books of the Old Testament] or the Book of Kings; for this part of Scripture will not be helpful to those of weaker intelligence at this hour; they should, however, be read at some other time."[5]

ship with another, but also a deeper comprehension of our own inner self."[6]

Basil once taught me, "The secret of your life begins and ends in silence. Your ability to be a friend resides there too. We live nearly on top of each other, here in the monastery, relying on each other in every way. And it works only because of silence."

"Silence is the school of love where you meet your Creator," he said. "It is in silence that you finally shut up the monkeys in your mind and the craziness in your life and listen to what the Father wants to say to your heart. We listen separately, but we are together."

Contemplatives remind me to appreciate the simple, little things—but also the complicated, enormous ones. "Lovers overflow with their loving until even their friends get a little bored, finding them so one-tracked and repetitious," Ambrose says. "But God isn't a lover in this sense. God's love is never turned off and on. God-as-Love cannot wait for exquisite moments in our lives when the mood is just right. God bombards us with love. Love is going on in us all the time."

"Then why don't I feel it more often?" I say to him.

"I don't know. Look to a friend."

5

SIT. PRAY. LISTEN.

to ripen
"push the tip of right thumb into fleshy part of left hand
several times"

—*A Dictionary of the Cistercian Sign Language*

Father Luke and I sat one afternoon in wooden lawn
chairs like a couple of lizards basking in the late October sun. It was one of those gorgeous New England
fall afternoons, and we took the occasion to escape the dark
comfort of the retreat house. I had never seen Luke as open
to answering questions as I did on that day, and so our conversation ranged over a variety of topics.

I had been wanting to ask Luke about the old men whom I
occasionally saw sitting in corners of the chapel all by themselves, motionless, in the dark. I'd been wondering about
them for years. They look as if they're sleeping or, frankly,
dead. Hours on end, they just sit there. On more than one
occasion while visiting the church, I have stayed long after

the liturgical office was over and everyone else had left, just to see if I could see them get up and go. No such luck.

"Tell me about the men I sometimes see sitting in the church after everyone else has gone," I asked.

"Who?" Luke said, seeming a bit puzzled.

"The men in the corners of the abbey chapel, sitting there for hours in the dark. I saw one just a few minutes ago, before I walked over here to meet you."

"I'll bet that that's Brother Bartholomew."

"Is he asleep?"

"No, he's definitely not sleeping," Father Luke replied. Luke always seemed to be honest with me, and so I felt confident pursuing this further.

"I thought that perhaps they fall asleep in prayer. They *do* seem to be the older monks."

"Oh no, I don't think so," Luke said. He wasn't exactly forthcoming—or perhaps I could not tell the difference between being cagey and being relaxed.

"Are they perfectionists, then? Are they trying to impress the others, or the abbot, with their sanctity—you know, by staying for prayer long after others have gone away?"

"I'm sure that's not it," he said, without a tinge of defensiveness. "A few decades ago, before we had private rooms, the church was often full with guys doing that because they had nowhere else to go. Back then, I suppose that there may have been a feeling of competitiveness in some of the guys from time to time, because you knew that others were watching. But even if that happened, a monk couldn't get away with that for very long at all.

"The men you see in there today are usually there because they've fallen in love," he continued. "Sometimes their hands are cold to the touch, as the guy has sort of gone out of himself."

"Oh, I see." But of course, I didn't.

"It can become almost addictive," Luke said. "It can sometimes become difficult to get them to move elsewhere, to do other things."

Poet George Herbert wrote, "Love is that liquor sweet and most divine, / Which my God feels as blood; but I, as wine!"

"There is an old understanding about monastic life that endures from the Middle Ages," Brother Alberic once told me. "People used to say, and monks used to say—you can find this in the early writings of Merton—that a monk is a man who has retired from the secular world in order to focus single-heartedly on saving his soul. Well, it's no wonder people once envied and resented us!"

"So, that's definitely not the case, now? There are no brothers here in the abbey who would look at it that way?" I asked.

"There had better not be. But no, I'm sure there are not."

"Why are you sure?"

"Because you can lose your soul inside these walls just as easily as you can on the outside. We're not here to save ourselves. God saves us. We're here because we feel that our calling is to these vows, to this way of life, and that this way of life is one way to help the world. Our prayers, our teachings, our place of respite, are intended to be a salve for others, but also a voice to God on behalf of others who may not have found that voice for themselves, yet."

Monastic life is a course in immersion. What a contrast it is to the usual language of modern life that has a way of distancing us from our words. We've learned from the culture to believe we cannot possibly comprehend what we say when we use religious words, or even worse, we cannot possibly mean them. In response to these challenges, modern theologians have become preoccupied with details that usually have very little to do with living a spiritual life. They work and think in a world that says you cannot mix the objective with the subjective: knowledge shouldn't be confused by an immersion in the subject matter.

People in churches hear the scriptures read every week, they use religious language in prayer and in conversation, and then theologians discuss the deeper meanings of those words. Rarely do the two meet.

I think the trouble comes from our assumptions. We assume the way to understand religious language is to study it, when in fact, understanding comes from using it, from putting it into action. As St. Aelred, a twelfth century Cistercian monk, said: "He who hasn't tasted, shouldn't tell."

Monastic ways of prayer have slowly made sense in my life. I have tried many types of embodied prayer—ways of praying beyond words—including journaling, drawing, mudras in sitting meditation, even some of the more charismatic Christian ways of using one's hands in prayer, but none of these allowed the spirit and words of my prayer to meet. It was in more monastic ways that I found my prayer home: praying the psalms in the Divine Office; *lectio divina* or spiritual reading during prayer; using beads to silently chart a course of repeated prayers; and centering prayer, as Basil Pennington tirelessly encouraged, twice a day for twenty minutes.

Father Basil and I talked about *lectio divina* on many occasions. "It seems too simple to be a spiritual practice," I remember saying to him once.

"It's simple to comprehend, but not as simple to do faithfully. Attending to it faithfully means becoming a closer friend with Christ. *Lectio* is another way of conversing with Christ. That's a mighty thing—mighty simple, yes, but mighty. You see? And in *lectio* you allow Christ, as it were . . . you shut you up to the point where you allow him to pick the topic, not you."

I don't usually shut up and sit still long enough to allow Christ to speak into my life. In fact, I usually approach my *lectio* and centering prayer as just two more items on my to-do list for the day.

Twenty minutes of prayer upon waking. Write. Breakfast. Shower. Kids off to school. Off to work. At night get the kids to bed, maybe watch TV. Clean up or wash dishes. Write. Brush teeth. *Lectio* for about fifteen minutes. Twenty minutes of prayer. Go to sleep.

"Resting in God" is what Gregory the Great called Christian contemplation. "It's all about friendship, Jon," Basil explained. "You don't schedule your friends like tasks, do you? And this isn't only your friend; this is your lover, your most intimate companion. You certainly wouldn't treat your lover as a task, would you?"

He didn't wait for me to respond. "No, of course you wouldn't," he continued with a smile. But it wasn't just a smile; he gave me a grin and looked wistfully up and to the right, as if he was remembering an affair or a weekend in Paris on his honeymoon. The look on Basil's face at those moments made it seem as if this celibate monk was scandalously in love with a woman somewhere. But of course, that wasn't it at all.

"Of course you wouldn't.

"You would settle down throughout the day, maybe not only morning and evening, with gratefulness and joy—an otherwise overused word—to simply be in the presence of your Lover." And he looked at me, raising his eyebrows.

"Yes," I answered.

⸻⸺⸻

To be a contemplative is not only to do and not do certain things, but it is a different worldview. Father Ambrose tried to explain this to me: "We are exiles, homeless. We are unsure of who we are, forever seeking to figure that out."

"You mean, 'strangers in a strange land'? That whole thing?" I asked.

"Yes, that's part of it. We are living in ways that seem to fit heaven more than earth sometimes. But you have to be careful too: we create this big false self all of the time, fooling even ourselves as to who we are."

"But, honestly, what other option do you have?" I asked.

"Well, I'll tell you, but it is a dark road." He went on, "We are homeless exiles, as I said, like in one of those strange science fiction stories. And what we should seek, I think, is who God says that we are."

"So, who does God say that you are?"

"That's just it; there is no 'I' in God. There is this beautiful and mysterious union that cannot even be described. I am forever seeking who God says I am."

He said it without a hint of self-confidence. It was a confession, not a teaching. And I wondered just how relevant it could be for my life in the *real* world.

Monks have always been counter-cultural in their worldview, decisions, and everyday habits. Never has a monk been hip. Their lives appeal to me for these very reasons—because they turn back the imagination to an era when perhaps it was easier to focus on what matters most.

What must it have been like to wake up in the morning in one of Saint Benedict's monasteries in sixth-century Italy? There were distractions back then, but not as many. We haven't progressed as much as we think, in other ways. In fact, we've probably regressed. That's what Father Ambrose was trying to explain. We think of ourselves as getting more done now, but think back to the days before electricity when people stayed home in the evenings and talked with each other. They read. They prayed. It was also the era before any transportation swifter than a horse. People necessarily moved more slowly, got less done of what we get done and more of what we don't. The word *multitasking* had not yet been invented.

"We know nothing new under the sun," Father Ambrose once told me, as we walked outside on an autumn day. "We prefer to believe we are doing far better than our ancestors or parents once did. We are able to fight more disease, more efficiently transport ourselves, and we know more than human beings have ever known before. Right?"

"Right."

An Unusual Trappist Custom

Visit a Trappist monastery church for a celebration of Holy Communion and you will experience an unusual custom they practice. The monk/priest who is presiding stands in the middle, facing the altar and the congregation, but then, all of the monks who are also priests gather around him and participate as well. During the liturgical moments of consecrating the bread and the wine, every priest raises his right hand in gesture toward the elements, as if each man is participating in the miracle that is occurring at that moment.

"But there is so much we have lost from what our ancestors once understood."

A monk's life is one of study and preparation, but not really of an academic kind. He knows that he's in school—his entire life is a process of being schooled—but that doesn't remotely mean he is studying without practice in real life. I sometimes think of their approach to faith through the metaphor of baseball's spring training. There is book study and examining the past, but it doesn't make much sense to stay in the video room. They have to take it out on the field.

I know I'm not the first evangelical Protestant who has eventually turned to Catholic methods of prayer, tired with my own attempts to be spontaneous. Praying according to ancient traditions can become the antidote to too much self in prayers that are full of "We just want to thank you, Lord . . ." and the other attempts to be conversational with the Almighty. When I hear the words "We just want to thank you, Lord . . ." my mind has already left the building. Coleridge's famous maxim about poetry is, I think, true about some forms of religion. I would simply change his first word, "poetry," to "religion": "~~Poetry~~ Religion—excites us to artificial feelings—makes us callous to real ones."

Still, the author of *The Cloud of Unknowing*—the most important mystical text for a Trappist—warns the young away from spiritual practices as well as study. You must not only be baptized, the anonymous author wrote, but you must also be regenerated or "mended" as Richard Rolle once put it. Then the qualities of charity and humility must be evident in your life. And even then, if you are a frivolous, selfish, or self-absorbed person—well, God help you! You'd be better off dead than studying the words and practice of Christian mystical prayer, he explains. This is serious stuff. Perhaps that's what makes monastic life so appealing and yet so often poorly imitated.

———∽∽∽———

The digital clock in my car read 4:47 and I was still about five minutes from the abbey. I had driven nearly three hours to get there; I had an appointment with Father Bernard set for 5:15 and I knew the gift shop closed at 5.

I greeted the brother behind the desk when I rushed into the shop. "I just need some jam before you close," I said. "They no longer carry it at my grocery store."

"They don't?" he asked.

"No. They stopped for some reason."

"Which store is that?"

I told him, and he wrote it down in a notebook. "I'll check on it," he said.

"I have to get up the hill to see Father Bernard," I explained. The clock on the wall read 5:10.

"When is your appointment?" the brother asked.

"Right about now, actually," I replied.

"Well then, you'd better hurry. Bernard is famous for his punctuality. I know that I wouldn't want to make him wait!" he chortled.

Turns out I wasn't late, and Father Bernard and I settled down in a couple of old swivel chairs in the monastery library at exactly 5:15 according to the clock on the table in front of me. I smiled to myself.

I was planning on seeing both Bernard and Luke this day. Underneath the basic similarities, they are as different as two men can be. Bernard is the precise and punctual one, while Luke is all soul and free spirit.

I wanted to ask them both the same basic question. Their answers were similar, but their approach very different. I said to Bernard, "Tell me how I, living my secular, Protestant life, can ever really understand your way of life."

He lit up with enthusiasm, and turned to a file folder he had prepared to give to me, which was lying on the table in front of us.

"Let me read to you," Bernard began. "Benedictine monk, Laurence Freeman . . . do you know him?" he asked, looking up.

"Yes, I've actually met him once."

Bernard looked pleased. "Well, Freeman once wrote about John Main, his teacher, saying: 'He taught that "every time you sit to meditate you enter into the tradition" because he had discovered for himself that tradition is a living, ever-evolving spiritual transmission in which individual experience continually merges with everything that has been experienced authentically by others. The inauthentic dissolves. The real remains and forms a collective wisdom in the operation of the Spirit. We can say that we have, in his words, found a "personal experience of the truths of our faith" when what transpires in us finds its completion and larger meaning in the catholic (universal) tradition.'[1] Suffice it to say that you can enter into this way of life, albeit in small doses, when you sit to pray," he concluded.

Bernard handed me the photocopied pages that he had just quoted.

Then he turned to the next page in the folder. He began again, "This is also an excellent article you should read. Thomas à Kempis spoke of 'the inward man' in *The Imitation of Christ*. Meister Eckhart, his near contemporary in Germany, preached about what we might call 'the inward God.' These are the two handfuls of prayer: attentiveness to the inward person—what we do, feel, sense—as well as attentiveness to God in our selves, bodies, spirits."

None of this really clicked for me. *I have enough to read*, I couldn't help thinking, even as I was grateful for the way he had prepared for our talk.

An hour later, I sat down in my familiar chair with Father Luke in the retreat house. How I have grown to love that chair! And I asked him the question I had asked Father Bernard: "Do you think it is possible for a layperson, and a Protestant like me, to have any real understanding of what your life is really like?"

Without pausing for a second, he shot back, "Absolutely!"

Absolutely? I was shocked. Even knowing Luke as I did, knowing his kindness and his decades of work as a confessor to laypeople and his hundreds of relationships with retreatants, listening to them for hours, I expected something very different. Other monks had said to me that they didn't think their lives would make sense to someone looking in from the outside. I could tell that they often felt as if they appeared to be gargoyles to the tourist, even though they were something much more beautiful to those who really knew them.

"Absolutely, you can," he added, seeing that I hadn't quite taken it in.

"The Christian who practices contemplative prayer and lives a more contemplative life has a very clear, but perhaps brief, understanding of what my life is all about," he said.

———— ✺ ————

Is he humoring me? I wondered.

In his biography of Thomas Merton, Fr. William Shannon wrote:

The monk is distinguished from other people (whose lives are also a search for God) by the fact that the monk gives himself exclusively and most directly in the seeking of God. Others seek God in the midst of responsibilities in society and family. Other (active) religious seek God by seeking to help others in their search for God. This does not mean that the monk's exclusive concentration on the seeking of God makes the monk a better person (or better Christian) than these others; it is simply that he treads a path that most others do not choose: not necessarily a higher or safer or more dedicated path, simply one he knows he is called to follow.[2]

And so I asked Luke, "Are you humoring me? Don't monks manage to keep themselves exclusively concentrated on God?"

"Of course not!" he shot back. "And we don't even pretend we do."

"Then what's different about you?" I said, with a grin.

"The same thing that I think is different about you—the ground of who you are, the place that you instinctively return to, your identity, in Christ."

"Maybe," I said.

"Prayer can also be very personal. We speak of locutions," Father Bernard said to me one day. I had to ask him what that meant. I don't think anyone had ever used the word with me before.

A locution is a message, a revelation. You may have seen a painting of St. Francis of Assisi praying in the mountains, the crucified icon of Christ hovering above him, and rays of light beaming into his body to create his stigmata wounds. St. Francis is receiving a locution in this painting.

"Most locutions are ordinary," Bernard said. "I'm not saying I'm some sort of special saint or something."

Most Christians don't talk about revelations anymore; even the cradle Catholic has often learned to doubt too much to think that "revelation" is a meaningful word anymore. And many Protestants run the other way as quickly as they can when interior visions are mentioned. That mystical stuff is "sketchy," as my teenage daughter would say.

Robert Hugh Benson, the son of an Archbishop of Canterbury who later converted to Catholicism, once explained how St. Teresa of Avila's revelations blended with what was otherwise a very practical life. Teresa realized early on in life "that there is but one thing in the world really worth pursuing—the knowledge of God; that this quest is one which verifies itself as it is pursued—that it increases, that is to say, the sense of reality in the soul that follows it, instead of, as the materialist thinks, leading to mere visionariness and abstraction—and that while on the one side its reality is so great as to make all else insignificant, on the other it must use images of created things in order to express itself; and that it develops rather than retards the administration of even the most practical concerns."[3]

Father Bernard's locutions are not always visual messages. Sometimes a locution comes in the form of a thought or idea with a divine origin. Bernard told me about two in particular.

"They come unexpectedly and they are always brief.

" 'Submit,' a voice said to me once as clear as day. I was walking in the church early in the morning. That was it.

"And then later, while walking on Mount Sinai outside of Jerusalem—I was privileged to spend several years in the Holy Land as a younger man—I heard unmistakably, 'God alone matters.' "

These were gifts to Bernard, and he knew it. "I don't mention this to many of the monks," he said. I felt honored. These verbal messages, heard by his ears (not just in his mind) "were like manna," he explained. Unusual and brief, but nourishing. "Those messages became what fueled in me what we in the monastic life call God-mindfulness," he said.

⦿⦿⦿

You won't often encounter a monk who claims to have had visions and auditory revelations from God. Such things are not usually the Trappist way. As *The Cloud of Unknowing* says, extraordinary mystical experiences are more often the product of something inside of ourselves, than of God.

"Still, I find many Christians will admit to it," Father Bernard said to me that day. "We admit it a bit sheepishly, sometimes."

"I have heard God speak to me," Basil Pennington remarked to me on another occasion. "There's nothing strange about it at all. I am quiet, listening for God's voice every day, and I often hear it in the quiet of my soul." Basil talked with God like a man talking to a friend—they were intimate friends, indeed. This is not the stuff of tale-telling or fantastic experiences.

Nearly a century ago, Evelyn Underhill said to a group of British clergy:

> We are drifting towards a religion which consciously or unconsciously keeps its eye on humanity rather than on Deity— which lays all the stress on service, and hardly any of the stress on awe: and that is a type of religion which in practice does not wear well. It does little for the soul in those awful moments when the pain and mystery of life are most deeply felt. It does not provide a place for that profound experience which Tauler called "suffering in God." It does not lead to sanctity . . . It does not fit those who accept it as adequate for the solemn privilege of guiding souls to God . . . In fact,

it turns its back on the most profound gifts made by Christianity to the human race.[4]

That ineffable reality to which we've dedicated our lives asks to be better known.

Luke and I were out walking one afternoon when he said to me, "A Christian is a link to the supernatural world, even more so than to the natural one. And how do we really link to the supernatural? Holy Communion and the sacraments. Prayer. Contemplation."

"Do you believe in the reality of a living God? How do you turn your belief into real understanding?" Luke continued, in the way he often says it to Protestant retreatants at the Abbey.

"There is an ineffable knowledge of God. It's a lost art, not a big secret. No one hid it anywhere.

"I'm not talking about trances and visions. I'm not talking about a gaze like the one found in French Quietism that was once deemed heretical—those were religious experiences just for the purpose of having an experience—no, I'm talking about what Teresa of Avila knew. She was a very practical woman. She said, 'Contemplation is the gaze of faith fixed on Jesus.' We don't know what she knew; I can tell you that much!"

I once knew a man named David who lived in a remote part of the Hudson Valley in New York. He was a meditator and the author of several popular books on meditation. We became fairly good friends over the course of several years.

David lived in a house high on a hill with his wife, a musician and also a meditator. They were old hippies who had become adept at meditation in ways that are comparable to what the

gurus of Eastern religions might do. You could see the result-
ing profoundly relaxed look on their faces. David and his wife
were able to go on long meditation retreats. They would often
take six months or longer full-time meditation retreats in exotic
places around the world. On other occasions, they would an-
nounce to those on their mailing list that they were shutting up
the house for six or nine weeks to do six- and nine-hour-long
sessions each day of intensive "sitting."

They must have inherited money, because earning a living
never seemed to get in the way of their practice. And David
promoted himself into what you'd have to call a *professional*
meditator. His classes were well attended and his books very
popular. But there was something that always bothered me
about it all.

There's a funny line in a Woody Allen movie about someone becoming so mellow (which was considered a valued trait
by some in the 1970s) that he might eventually turn to rot. I
couldn't help but think of that possibility sometimes when
I was with David. He had cultivated an other-worldliness
that unnerved those of us in this world. His *mellowness*
was not contrived—it was real—but that doesn't mean it
was healthy or even something to be imitated. Meditation
seemed to have become for him at times a drug or a veneer—
a spa, a loss of vitality. And his professional approach was
like the difference between the art of a weaver and the art
of a spider: the first is a practiced skill, while the second is
a natural grace.

I've made my own mistakes in trying monastic prayer. I used
to think of it as a variation of high definition listening. In fact,
meditators in every tradition will tell you that stripping away
noise, calming a busy "monkey mind," and deep listening are

all essential. I've tried that sort of thing but never felt that I was making a connection. Being quiet wasn't enough.

I described this to Father Basil one afternoon and he said to me, "To emphasize listening is to make a mistake. We are there to give ourselves to the Lord. Listening can be seeking something for self. It can mislead people, leaving them looking for some experience of God or making too much of something coming from their own imagination.

"When you are truly with God and nothing else, you aren't doing anything. Nothing measurable is happening."

Father Basil used to teach centering prayer to people of all sorts. He would sit with families with little children, with business people. He would show them how to do it for twenty minutes a day twice a day, and then they would ask questions.

"What should I be thinking about while I'm praying?"

"Nothing."

"Then what am I doing?"

"You are being quiet, and settling in silence to spend time with your Creator."

Like me, people would sit there puzzled, expecting more from the answers.

Father Luke once explained, "Even though sitting with God in prayer is a gift, it is still something to work at. If you do," he explained, "I guarantee that you will find happiness—and in things that are different from what the world tells you are the places to find meaning."

"Arise without delay," St. Benedict writes in the Prologue to his Rule. "Let us open our eyes to the Divine light and attentively hear the Divine voice, calling and exhorting us daily."

Like running water settling into pools, life's meaning comes through more clearly when I am consciously in God's presence.

The big questions that trouble me because they don't have clear answers all fade away in importance. My favorite seminary professor of blessed memory, Paul Holmer, first introduced me to the Austrian philosopher, Ludwig Wittgenstein, twenty years ago. To paraphrase Wittgenstein, "Anyone who understands me correctly will ultimately understand that all of the logical distinctions I have discussed are ultimately without meaning, nonsensical. You must use these big questions like a ladder—and when you get to the top, throw the ladder away. You no longer need it. You will only see the world correctly when you transcend the big questions. And then, you arc silent."[5]

Contemplation is a gift. You can't achieve it. The psalmist sang, "He brought me to an open space. He rescued me because he delighted in me" (Ps. 18:20). The person who could sing such words with authenticity is one who must have known an intimacy with God. And such intimacy is not easily felt or understood.

The man in deep contemplative prayer—like those monks alone for hours in the church at St. Joseph's Abbey—looks almost dead. There is something frightening about putting your life into the hands of a living God. Anyone who tells you that God is all cuddly love simply doesn't know God firsthand. I like how the French writer, Leon Bloy, put it nearly a century ago: "God wants everything, He requires everything, and one cannot escape Him.—'We are sold to God,' my wife said to me, 'we are caught in His net, and we know this net cannot be broken.' O terrible joy, that begins with a cry of distress!"[6] This terrible joy is part of the contemplative's experience.

———⟨∞⟩———

Several years ago, in February 2004, I was feeling everything but union with God. My wife and I were having some serious troubles, the sort of stuff that you don't feel comfortable talking about even with close friends; my work was increasingly difficult; I had several health problems that had never come up before; and I was angry.

At such times, the *idea* that God is love, as told in scripture, church, and by many of my friends, doesn't help at all. Hymnal-like platitudes about God's loving me actually damage God's image in my eyes at times like these. Some people have little context in their lives for understanding a godly love—they don't experience it. That's not exactly me, but at this point in my life I hear what is being said more than I experience it firsthand.

I sit down with Father Ambrose to talk about love, to ask him about love. He rubs his hands together as if he is about to eat a luscious piece of cake.

"You don't always feel it, Jon," he begins. "Those times when you do are precious. They are precious and marvelous." He looks up at the ceiling.

After a long minute, Ambrose continues, "I think that the point of all Christian revelation boils down to this: God says, Please stop trying to escape Mercy. Stop running from my merciful love."

"I'm not running anywhere. I'm hurt," I say with a healthy dose of bitterness.

"I know," he says, "but God didn't do this, didn't stop loving you.

"Divine love is full of mercy to its core. It's grace. You cannot buy it, earn it, achieve it—and you can't command it, deserve it. But you have it if you need it. Until you realize that you need it, the love of God is almost defeated—like those raindrops that cannot wet the too-dry soil. But our Father keeps raining, endlessly showering his merciful love on us, until one day, somehow, it seeps in and we finally know who we are and who he is. Or until one day, suddenly and quietly, by the pressure of this love in you, you finally surrender and the water of his life soaks into the root of your life."

"But I haven't gone anywhere," I say urgently. "Where have I gone? I'm right here."

"Sit. Pray. Listen. Don't stop doing that, no matter how you feel. God's love keeps tapping our soil, asking us to be his sinners, to let his mercy in—his gratuitous, undeserved love."

6

WORK AND PLAY

flower
"hold tips of right thumb, forefinger, and middle finger together; then bring them to nose as though smelling them"

—*A Dictionary of the Cistercian Sign Language*

For ten to twelve hours a day, we aren't doing anything specific," Father Luke once told me. "I usually read the daily paper, I keep informed about world events on the Web, I write long letters to people."

"Really?" I said, inarticulately. "You mean cloistered doesn't mean away from the world?"

"It once was that our abbots would forbid too many letters, forbid novels, cassettes, magazines, newspapers, that sort of stuff—anything that might turn our minds away from our cells and God. That's not the way anymore.

"In fact, I'm more informed than most of the diocesan priests that I know who come here on retreat. From the top of a hill, you can have a better view of things."

Contemplatives set out to strip their lives of what's unnecessary—owning things, gaining power or position at work, status—which sometimes means that they have more time to enjoy what the rest of us have little time for. This isn't exactly their work, but it is their way of life and sometimes the two become confused.

Undoubtedly, there is a seriousness about any monastery. You couldn't drive up the driveway of one and not quickly catch on that you are supposed to be reverent, quiet, respectful—and for that reason, some people react as if they are still children being hushed in church. It is easy to feel a reaction to the environment of a monastery. You may feel compelled to stand up and shout, if only to see what everyone else would do about it. Conversely, some of the more devout monastery visitors also react like children with their excessive piety in the presence of the monks, as if that's what might be expected. Either way, many people's first responses to the piety and sobriety of the monastery is a childish one.

Despite or because of their earnest approach to life, nowhere but in a monastery is it clearer to me that play is also serious. True playfulness is not an avoidance of responsibility. It's not negative. The best play is characterized by a true spirit and feeling of freedom.

Perhaps it's ironic that cloistered monks play so well. They are not exactly free, are they? They have taken vows of serious commitment and as a result their freedoms to move away, to enter into certain relationships, to obtain and possess things, have all been curtailed. But as I've found, these curtailed freedoms actually have the reverse effect of freeing them to uncover and express their truer selves.

Most monks I know laugh more often than other people, even though St. Benedict's Rule tells them not to laugh easily. I think this is because they understand their own silliness. When you're a monk you spend little or no time and effort disguising yourself. Think of those times throughout a typical day when you stand in front a mirror, or ponder what to wear, or think about the right words to say. Monks have little occasion for these things. As a result, they see more clearly the awkwardness of the human situation. Those aspects of my life that I try to cover up, or mask—appearance problems, image maintenance, sham confidence—actually reveal the human being for what it is: fractured and frail. What infant species is more vulnerable than a human? Horses can in most cases walk and even run in the first hours after birth. But not us, not even close. As adults, we become adept at overcoming this basic frailty, but in the monastery, frailty is actually encouraged.

A monk is to be humble, and in his humility, he finds humor. As St. Benedict says, "By means of his very body [he] always shows his humility to all who see him: that is, in work, in the oratory, in the monastery, in the garden, on the road, in the field, or wherever he may be . . . With head always bent down and eyes fixed on the earth, he always thinks of the guilt of his sins and imagines himself already present before the terrible judgment seat of God."[1] It may not seem like much to laugh at, but it can be. Personal humility combined with God's judgment can seem at times like preparing for a typhoon by purchasing an umbrella. There's not much to do but laugh.

The brothers can be surprisingly hip when it comes to contemporary culture. It's not uncommon for the monks to circulate DVDs between them, and then for the jokes to become part of their cultural literacy. *The Simpsons* has been one example of this. Homer Simpson once described his faith as "the one with all the well-meaning rules that don't work in real life." Anyone who has watched the television show more than once knows that Homer is probably incapable of any epiphany whatsoever—that's what makes him so funny. We realize how incapable we are too of real epiphanies. Still, Homer falls into one from time to time.

At the beginning of *The Simpsons Movie*, America's family is walking briskly to church, running late. Just as they approach the front door, Homer says in a loud voice, not realizing that the windows are all open and that everyone inside can overhear, "These pious morons are too busy talking to their phony-baloney God!"

"I've felt that way more than once," Father Luke said with a wry grin one afternoon when we were chuckling about Homer and Bart.

The lesson of *The Simpsons* seems to be that we usually create our own problems, our own crises, and then, with a little help from each other and—yes, from God—we can find the way out of our messes. At a crisis moment in the film, Homer riffles through a copy of the Bible while in a church pew, his family all around him, and he exclaims, "This book doesn't have any answers!"

Homer is, of course, all of us. That's why his bumbling, his outbursts, his desire for simple answers, and his selfishness are so funny—because we can imagine ourselves doing the same. At the film's end, Homer indeed saves the day; Grandpa yells to him, "What are you doing?" And Homer replies, "Risking my life to save people whom I hate for reasons I don't understand!" Sounds like an outrageous version of what one might hear from a monk living in community.

"Living together, as close as we do, can be funny almost without trying," Father Luke told me as we sat in the library. "We stumble on top of each other sometimes at work. We make each other sick, because we live so closely together. You know, there's no escape around here. You'd better like people if you want this to work out for you!"

"The monastic life forces us," Father Luke said, "to figure ourselves out with God.

"The only real distractions available are within us—or perhaps when we become preoccupied with the quirks of another monk. But you are deliberately alone for much of your life, and especially on feast days and holidays. You have to learn how to use your time well. You read. You walk. There isn't much recreation just for recreation's sake."

They tell me that it's not the rules and vows that are the most difficult aspect of monastic life, but living in community and in obedience. Imagine that another adult has the power to change your job and responsibilities without notice on a Monday morning; to ask you to move from one place to another; to withhold things that you've grown to appreciate. Monks have this sort of relationship with their abbots. Their vows demand it, even though abbots are more likely, these days, to consult with their monks rather than give orders. And it is this reality of their lives that often yields a profound light-heartedness toward the stuff, things, and power of everyday life. They've given them up.

"The rules and the obedience can bring contentment rather than difficulty, at least if you have the right sort of personality for it," Luke said with a smile.

Active and Contemplative Orders

There are many ways to distinguish one group of monks from another. There are differences between Eastern and Western monasticism. There are even Protestant monks in Anglicanism, Lutheranism, and United Methodism. There are Third Order members of monastic groups, and oblates. These last are not monks at all; they are people who want to associate with a nearby abbey for spiritual reasons. Something that often escapes people's notice is that some of the largest religious orders are not, in fact, monks. Friars (called to a life of poverty and service) are not monks (called to a life of prayer and devotion), and monks are not friars. Friars are often called the *active* orders, and include four groups: Franciscans, Dominicans, Carmelites, and Augustinians.

The lack of material things is also a sort of freedom. How free it is not to own things! I have come to know a portion of that truth in my own life. I once owned a house, but no longer; I used to collect rare books, but no more; and I'm grateful. St. Francis of Assisi used to teach his brothers that if they owned things, they'd have to worry about them, perhaps defend them, and if they had to defend them, they'd end up using violence and behaving in ways that they'd rather not. To live poorer than is required by your resources is one injunction that Jesus gave his first disciples, and I've found that to do it is not a virtue; instead, it is both practical and rewarding.

Living poorer compared to the rest of the world around you can bring with it blessings and gratefulness for the smaller things. Hospitality takes on fresh meaning: to give to others what you rarely give to yourself. Plenty of work goes into doing hospitality well. I've eaten many an extravagant meal in the monastery that reminds me of the following prayer poem of St. Brigid of Kildare:

I would like an enormous lake of the finest ale
for the King of kings.
I would like a table of the most succulent foods
for the family of heaven.
Let the ale be made from the fruits of faith,
and the food from forgiving love.

I would welcome the poor to my feast,
for they are God's children.
I would welcome the sick to my feast,
for they are God's joy.
Let the poor sit with Jesus at the highest place,
and may the sick dance with the angels.

God bless the poor,
God bless the sick,
and bless our human race.

God bless our food,
God bless our drink,
Everyone, O God, embrace.[2]

Play and work, of course, help each other along. Trappist monks do not live practical lives, as the other so-called *active* orders do. Franciscan and Dominican friars' lives are designed to stay busy most of the time. They preach and teach and write and administrate. In contrast, Cistercians and Carthusians and Camoldolese, are intended to be more restful, not active and not exactly passive—somewhere between the two. Not preoccupied. Their charism, or special ministry, is to love. If that sounds a bit fuzzy to you, well, I think it's supposed to. But living contemplatively usually means being at rest more than being busy. This is the hardest part for me about trying to live more monastically outside the cloister. I like work too much, and allow work to define me.

Trappists *do* work, and sometimes very hard, but for short periods of time. A monk will tell you that daily physical work is necessary for every person if for no other reason than to allow your restless mind to sit still for a while. While the body is moving the mind is forced to settle down.

I know a monk who writes beautiful homilies, presides over Mass, and gives profound retreats, and yet he still repairs the electrical systems of the abbey each afternoon. I know others who study very little and have almost no taste for theology. They create works of art such as pottery, bonsai trees, and icons instead. Others not only make fruit jam and farmer's cheese and liturgical vestments, but they market them to retailers as well.

Work is discreet in the monastery. I often see the men in work clothing, but rarely do I witness the work itself. Brother Samuel, who gardens and tends some of the small animals and hens, will occasionally be seen carrying a box of tools. I once saw him carrying the wooden box awkwardly, as a priest would process with a monstrance. Work can be its own reward.

Work was made holy by St. Benedict in his Rule. Before Benedict in the sixth century, work was the stuff done by people who had no choice but to do it. In the Roman Empire, slaves were acquired to do as much of the physical work as possible, and getting one's hands dirty with manual labor was seen as a curse one was born into. But with St. Benedict, work became prayer, not to be distinguished from other kinds of mental prayer. Your hands are praying while building a table.

A Plot to Murder Benedict

Not all of Benedict's monks were enamored with his new emphasis on work. We know of a murderous plot on the part of the monks of one of Benedict's monasteries, Vicovaro. They had convinced the famous abbot to oversee their monastery in addition to his own, but then sometime later, decided they weren't too happy about the rigors and expectations that he brought with him. One night, some of the brothers poisoned Benedict's cup of wine. It is said that when the abbot blessed his food, the cup shattered, alerting him that it was tainted. Benedict rebuked the men and left the monastery, refusing to be their abbot any longer.

Your body is praying not only in kneeling before the altar, but in sweating in the fields to produce daily bread too.

I once said to a novice who was assisting me with a computer problem at a monastery, "Thanks very much for your help. It's great to have an expert around!" And he replied to me, almost shocked, "Expert? I don't know very much at all. In fact, I was just given this job a few months ago. I do what I can."

For a monk, real work is not a career or a way to become proficient at something. It is more like a diversion, because prayer is so intense that a monk needs a few hours of rest from it each afternoon. This break is a period of time each day when he can help his brothers by doing a particular task around the house that he has been assigned to do. He is supposed to do it with his utmost concentration and effort, but that doesn't mean it in any way defines him.

"Sometimes we are all given the same job," Father Luke explained to me one morning. "I remember when we were cultivating those hills you see out there." We were sitting in folding chairs on a bright, sunny day, facing the gentle green hills surrounding St. Joseph's Abbey in Massachusetts. "Every able brother was out taking turns bailing hay. In fact, Basil narrowly escaped getting seriously hurt one afternoon. He was the strongest of us all, you see, and he could throw those hay bails far up on the back of the truck, farther than the rest of us. But one afternoon, Basil was working so vigorously that he almost didn't realize his work smock—we all wore them back then—got caught in the manure spreader. The smock was not only torn off, but it grabbed him into the contraption, as well.

"We stopped wearing those long work smocks, intended to replicate our monastic garb, after that happened. Now it's blue jeans for those at work."

"But you don't always work together," I said.

"No, in fact we usually don't, these days. Only in times of big projects, such as a construction project, does that tend to happen. Now, each monk has his job, except for those like me who basically live in the infirmary because we're so old!"

Specific Jobs

The medieval monastery was a synchronized workplace of diverse responsibilities. Each member of the house was given a different responsibility by the abbot, as he discerned the skills as well as personal needs of each man. Each monk was required to accept the job given to him; he was then known as an *obedientiary*, which means, "one who follows his obedience." These jobs included the porter (keeper of the front door), the cellarer (coordinator of all food and drink), the sacrist (care for the church building), the infirmarer (care for the sick), and the novice master (teacher of students). Each *obedientiary* took an oath to the abbot to work diligently, keep quiet about the work, and never slander about someone else and his job.

The flipside of hard work in the monastery is the rest of a monk. "We are forced to be at rest, to avoid busyness. We are forced to have more time to reflect than a person would ever naturally be able to handle," Father Luke said to me one day.

"That's an interesting way to put it. It sounds all good to me. You mean that you don't enjoy having less to do?" I asked, somewhat naively.

"It is another form of work, I tell you. And you have to be called to it, I believe. It is a grace from God and it is a gift to the world," he said, "when used for him."

"No one else in the Church is given this gift of leisure like the Trappists are," Luke continued. "For five or six hours a day we have nothing we have to do. Parish priests, God bless them, don't have time to read theology or papal encyclicals—or even for much daily prayer. They are just too busy."

"So how does your leisure and time for prayer help them?" I asked.

"Our life is like a fulcrum, it raises the world," Luke said. "The gift of contemplation is never just for oneself, but for the world—or as Pope Benedict says, for the body of Christ which is the same as humanity."

I was processing what Luke said before I registered that he had begun speaking again.

"Write this down, Jon," he said, getting my attention. "Think of it like this: we are the part of the ship under the water. The ballast would be off if we were off."

"Okay, so what is your advice for that parish priest who is too busy? What can he do? We shouldn't all come to the abbey and become Trappists, right?"

"No, it's not the right calling for every person. Not that we're better than those who aren't called to it. That's not what I mean.

"Here's what I hope you do, and what I try to guide others to do. You can be like a monk. All you need is a moment with God each day, but you must find that moment.

"Find time for private prayer.

"Read. Find time for at least some of that too.

"And then sit and think. Find time to just sit and think. Otherwise, your work, whatever it be, will be shallow."

———— ∽∾∾∽ ————

Father Ambrose was a novice under Thomas Merton at Gethsemani Abbey in the 1950s. He once recalled what it was like to learn theology from Merton. Ambrose was young and earnest, and schooled in the Latin of pre-Vatican II Catholicism. Merton had asked him to write an essay on the meaning of the Incarnation, and Ambrose filled it with Latin, explaining fine nuances of theology supported by lengthy quotes from the Church Fathers. Merton read his work and marked it up with a red pen.

According to Ambrose, "I could hardly see my original anymore, it was so covered in red! Almost every word, it seemed, was marked through.

"He had written at the top: 'Say it with your own words!'"

This story reminded me of something one of my seminary professors once told me. He had taught for thirty years at Yale Divinity School and tired easily of the more obsequious among his Ivy League students. One morning, my professor was leaving the Divinity School chapel on a lovely morning. The service had been inspiring, full of soaring music. A visiting choir had sung glorious Gregorian chant. He said to the students who were walking beside him, "How beautiful that was!"

And one of the young men replied, "Yes, but only if we can benefit from the Latin text."

"If you can catch *Laud*, you'll do just fine," my professor replied.

That's saying it with your own words!

One afternoon, Father Luke and I wanted to go for a walk. But as we began, the temperature seemed to drop at our feet, and we retreated back indoors.

"I'm still trying to understand a vow of stability," I said, as we jogged inside. "First of all, what exactly does it mean, to vow stability? Are you not allowed to go anywhere without permission?"

"Yes, I suppose that that's it," Luke said, "but a vow is a positive promise, not a negative thing. I have vowed a commitment to this place, to these men.

"And I'll tell you, I'm not very interested in going other places. When you love your family and your place, you probably become more settled."

"But you do travel occasionally, right?" I asked.

"Yes, in fact I give an annual retreat for a group of nuns in the Southwest. I'm scheduled to go there next month. I love them and I enjoy doing it, but I'm not at all anxious to leave."

I often feel so very opposite to this that I had to probe deeper. I love to travel, to go places. Some people yearn for a hearth of their own; I'd rather have my suitcase. I almost enjoy the feeling of homelessness. Still, most of the images of God seem to be on Luke's side. Referring to where the creation story says God began to sweep over the face of the void, as a wind over water, the Puritan poet John Milton wrote in *Paradise Lost*: "Dove-like (thou) sat'st brooding on the vast Abyss." Our images are usually of God sitting, thinking, brooding. The psalmists refer again and again to God's "holy hill"—not his running brook or eroding banks. There are psalms with references to taking refuge in God: "When the foundations are being destroyed, what can the righteous do? The LORD is in his holy temple; the LORD's throne is in heaven" (Ps. 11:3–4). But then there are others with prayers of God's people asking God to wake up, to move on our behalf: "Stand up, O LORD, in your wrath; rise up against the fury of my enemies. Awake, O my God" (Ps. 7:6). Finally, there are occasions when the psalmist is clearly frustrated by the stillness of God: "Answer me when I call, O God, defender of my cause; you set me free when I am hard-pressed; have mercy on me and hear my prayer" (Ps. 4:1).

That's me, I thought. The monastery, according to St. Benedict, is a place for the weary to rest. And then it is a place for the weary to stop their wandering and traveling. To become still. Always in a monk's life, prayer calls him back from his work to rest.

"How does a vow of stability relate to who God is? Is God to be found more in being still than in being active?" I asked.

Father Luke often looks to the side, to his right or left, as he is preparing to answer one of my questions. He doesn't look up or down, as if he doesn't know the answer or as if he might tell me an untruth, but he looks to the side. What he's searching for is something from the past, an example or an experience that he can relate to me.

He looked to his right and said, "Thomas Keating used to talk of 'temporary professions' like the Buddhists have. Professions that last for perhaps five years or ten years. We also have residency programs where a man comes and lives among us as one of us with the blessing of the abbot for only three months, or six months.

"But the length of time doesn't matter that much. And the stay-put-ness is something to be learned. It's like a habit, really."

"So what *is* important, then?"

"Total self-giving. That's the truest imitation of God, and I think it is simply easier to accomplish through stability and some level of commitment," he concluded.

———⚬⚬⚬———

"Idle hands are the devil's workshop." This old saying dates back at least to Geoffrey Chaucer and then perhaps to St. Jerome. "If the devil catch a man idle, he'll set him at work," chronicled Thomas Fuller in his 1732 book of proverbs. I've read many a novel and seen many a movie that depict monks getting themselves into trouble.

I asked Father Basil, at a time when he was the abbot of a Trappist monastery, "If your day includes so much idle time, are you ever concerned that giving monks permission to spend hours in silent prayer and solitude might lead them to open their minds and hearts to other, less edifying, possibilities?"

We were standing in the hallway of the retreat house. Basil was so tall that he was always ducking as we walked in and out meeting rooms and through doorways. "Of course it's possible," he said. "We're like you. We're not spiritual supermen."

I've come to see how it is possible, sometimes and in some situations, to arrange my life more like a monk, living outside the monastery. Arranging things so that I have less that I have to do and more time for what Father Luke calls "holy leisure." To work hard, but to let it own me less and less. To make time to rest and to play. "To rest but not to be idle," as Father Luke says. And to give up care for little things, for events in the present and future that I cannot control, anyway.

"Remember the parable that our Lord tells of the foolish bridesmaids," Dom Basil said to me one day.

"I don't really remember," I said.

"Five of the young women went out to meet the bridegroom and they planned ahead, bringing extra oil for their lamps. Five others did not plan ahead. The bridegroom was late, he was delayed, and all ten women eventually fell asleep in their waiting for him. Doesn't *that* sound familiar—both the inordinate waiting we sometimes do, *and* the falling asleep!

"Anyway," he continued, "at midnight the bridegroom arrives. The five foolish ones had lamps that were going out and they couldn't see their way; they had to go and buy oil and so, missed the bridegroom. 'Keep awake therefore' the Lord said of those women. But it isn't falling asleep that did them in—for all ten of the women fell asleep. We *all* fall asleep."

"What was it, then?" I asked.

"Keep your focus on meeting the Bridegroom. Do what it takes. That's all that really matters."

7

UNLEARNING AMBITION
AND ORIGINALITY

to unload
"place back of right hand on left shoulder, then move it forward several times with quick motion"

> —*A Dictionary of the Cistercian Sign Language*

By 2007, I had been visiting off and on with Father Luke for more than five years. He was old enough to be my grandfather. On the surface, our lives could not have been more different. Raised Catholic, Luke entered the monastery as he was turning twenty. He had never married or relied on a paycheck, and couldn't possibly understand the life of a working husband and father. Or so I thought. It turns out that he could and he did. He saw right through me.

"Let's go somewhere cool," he said to me one day. I had come to talk with him on a hot summer afternoon. He took me to a room adjoining the infirmary with efficient air conditioning. The quarters were cramped, with books and shelving all around, but we had enough room to stretch out and relax, while the sun baked everything outside.

"If you want to deepen your experience of our life I think you need to unlearn some things," he began.

"What do you mean?" I asked, surprised at his directness.

"Habits. The way you think about your life and how you do certain things. I probably would call them preoccupations rather than habits. And I don't know if they preoccupy you very much; but they preoccupy most people," he explained.

"What are they?"

"Ambition and originality," Luke concluded.

"I'm not supposed to want either of those things?"

"For their own sakes, no. And undoing the ways you seek after them is a key to understanding this life of ours."

"I want to do well in my work, in my relationships. That's good . . . right?" I said to Luke. I was confused by this conversation.

"He's very ambitious—that's what we say about someone to compliment them, right? Well, it is true, people who work hard, who try hard, are applauded and rewarded. But I'll tell you: nothing could be worse here. Ambition puts *you* in the center. When you are in the center of things, other things are pushed out. And there is no greater danger to the contemplative life than narcissism."

By this time in our relationship, Luke knew I had decided to write a book about him and other monks. Pointedly, he said, "Write that down, Jon." Of course I did.

An hour later, as I was preparing to leave, Luke said, "Read John Cassian."

The French monk, John Cassian, lived in the fifth century. Cassian became a monk in the Holy Land and lived for a while in the Egyptian desert before settling back in his native

France and founding two monasteries near Marseilles. His message to his fellow monks was to point out the vanity of the secular world, the meaningless posturing and pomp that fills much of daily life.

Monks aim to balance what they call caring with not caring. Cassian taught them how. He wrote about the dangers of *accidie* in Latin, or *akedia* in Greek, which literally means "negligence" or "not caring," often translated as "sloth." The monk who gives in to *akedia*, Cassian says, is often unhappy, dissatisfied, sluggish, restless, lethargic, in a funk of malaise. He will have lost the desire to be with God; he will feel that it's all for naught. Cassian also speaks of *akedia* somewhat ominously, sounding almost like the writer of a Victorian ghost story: it is "especially disturbing to a monk about the sixth hour, like some fever which seizes him at stated times, bringing the burning heat of its attacks on the sick man at usual and regular hours . . . There are some of the elders who declare that this is the *midday demon* spoken of in the ninetieth Psalm"![1]

Yes, I had to look that one up. What was numbered 90 in the Latin psalter of the early Middle Ages is number 91 in our Bibles, today. Psalm 91:5–6 is what Cassian was referring to: "You will not fear the terror of the night, or the arrow that flies by day, or the pestilence that stalks in darkness, or the destruction that wastes at noonday."

To suffer from *akedia* is to be wounded by a shaft of a passion that causes our souls to go to sleep, says Cassian. It's like a certain kind of spiritual deadness or inertness. A monk is supposed to care—to care intensely about many things: prayer, the community of his brothers, his own spiritual development and growth in Christian virtue.

But there's a rub. A monk isn't supposed to care too much. I've bumped up against this in monastic spirituality again and again: care but don't over-care.

113

In Cassian, there's the sense that fleeing the wiles of *akedia* includes winnowing down to what's necessary. He tells his fellow-monks: stop dreaming of all of the things you could do, the spiritual books and gadgets you need, the pilgrimages you could take. Be content. Don't care about what you shouldn't care about. Care intensely, but only for the pearl of great price.

A few months later, I sat down with Father Luke to ask him more about caring and not-caring, unlearning ambition and originality.

"Don't be over-involved with your self. It's easy to do," he said.

"How do I know what's over-involved and what's healthy regard?" I asked.

"As a test, tell a man that his relative has just died, or that some other tragedy has occurred. What are his first thoughts? 'I hardly even knew her.' 'I'm not sure if I can get off work for the funeral.' 'Wow, I was just in that city last month; that could have happened to me!'"

He became very animated. "The narcissistic man cannot hear or see other people, or God."

I have my own measure of narcissism, I thought to myself. I've often made care almost into a religion of its own. Caring for my kids to the point of worrying when they cross the street without me. Caring about paying the mortgage to the point where I become stingy. Perhaps it's the Puritan in me, but too much caring has sometimes meant hoarding, perfectionism, over-working, and a general lack of faith.

On a recent Fourth of July celebration in our small Vermont town, this lesson came home to me in a rush. Everyone comes out, rain or shine, for the fireworks. There are people whom I see only there, from one year to the next. A fireworks display requires darkness, and that has become a problem for me because my kids no longer stay near me on our picnic blanket. When we arrived for the fireworks that year, my teenage daughter found one or two of her friends within half a minute, and disappeared into the chaos. "Meet me back here, as soon as it's over!" I yelled, not even sure if she heard me.

There is no other time of year when I would have allowed my only daughter, my joy, to wander into an unknown, where hundreds of other teenagers are doing I-don't-know-what in the darkness, and I am left to wait and wonder.

A couple years ago, I wouldn't even have allowed her to run off like that on the Fourth of July. *Why did I allow it this time?* As most parents know, I didn't *allow* it; I didn't really have a choice. But there came a time—not very long ago—when I simply had to learn to let go. I would have been happy if the kids sat quietly by my side forever. "May I, Dad?" "Would you like to go for a walk, Dad?" But it doesn't quite work that way anymore.

God has shown me I am unable to keep my daughter by my side and that I shouldn't try. God wants me to gradually let go. Just when I thought I was a strong father, up crop small, new ways that I must become weak.

My daughter was perfectly fine that evening. In fact, she met me back at the spot where she had left, within ten minutes of the end of the fireworks. Christ walks with her, and he is better for her than I will ever be.

On another rainy day several weeks later, Father Luke and I sat in our usual wood-paneled meeting room in the retreat house. There is not a crucifix on the wall, as there would always be in one of the sleeping rooms. But there are several sentimental paintings by unknown artists, the sort that people pick up at estate sales: one Road to Emmaus, another of a French village scene with kids in tattered clothing in the foreground, and another of what looks to be a hero of some sort astride his horse.

I arrived on this particular day with a heavy heart for some troubles my son was going through. I told Luke all about them, and how my boy was growing into a man and trying to figure out how to make the transition.

"He's a perfectionist," I told Luke, "which is part of his problem. He expects everything to be perfect. He does well at most things, and I think he annoys his friends because he's too perfect."

Luke knew exactly what I was talking about from firsthand experience.

"Like your son, Jon, most of us here start out as perfectionists," he said.

He saw my look of surprise. *Really?* I was saying with my face.

"Oh yes. It's another form of ambition run amok."

"So how is it that you don't drive each other nuts?" I asked him.

Luke laughed out loud. "I'm not sure, but we usually don't. I often say that for that very reason we know that God exists. God is present here, that's why we don't fight with each other all the time, and that's why community works."

There are perfectionist monks, just as there are perfectionist accountants, mothers, and school teachers. There are monks who want nothing more than to do everything perfectly, and to show their abbots that they are accomplishing amazing things.

But just as an accountant might be misunderstood, the motives of a monk are sometimes, as well. Brother Anthony, for instance, suffered from narcolepsy throughout his life. "That's why he worked so hard," Father Luke told me. "He baked bread every single day. And he always read while walking, you know, to keep himself alert. If you didn't know any better, you'd have thought he was doing those things to be more industrious than the rest of us. He wasn't."

I don't feel expectations of perfectionism when I'm visiting a monastery. Most of the monks I know know better than to aim for perfection. "A tricky balance," Father Luke said, "because we need to not act like converts even though our work is to continuously be converting."

"Living as a monk—and I believe you can do that, at least in part, outside the cloister—is not a crushing obligation," Luke said.

"You can do it," he added, "as long as you don't mind putting away ambition for money, power, and reputation. God doesn't want it, and your brother monks frankly don't care whether you have it or not," he concluded.

"There is nothing that made our abbot, Thomas Keating, more leery of a young monk than ambition," Father Luke told me once.

"There is no greater obstacle to contemplation," he continued, "and it is an obstacle to union with God, because a unitive life is entirely a gift. You can't produce it on your own, no matter how hard you work at it."

Perhaps this is why the author of *The Cloud of Unknowing* called the early stages of contemplation, "blind intent stretching to God." It can feel like banging your head against a wall in order to open a door—try as you might, trying and ambition are not the keys—only to discover that the door opens out rather than in.

When Thomas Merton and Thomas Keating joined the Trappists in the 1940s, they were an order of strict adherents to the law: the laws of being in the Order of Cistercians of the Strict Observance. The men slept on thin straw beds and wore woolen cowls even on the hottest summer days. They woke earlier and went to bed earlier than they do now. They were severe on themselves in ways that they learned from their medieval forebears.

It was in the 1950s when Keating was suffering from tuberculosis that he first had time away from this sort of legal activism. As any old Trappist today knows, it was Keating who rediscovered the ancient contemplative roots of the Cistercian way. He spent the better part of two years in a hospital trying to recover from his illness, and it was then and there that he first read John of the Cross. While he read, away from the hustle, busyness, and perfectionism of monks in the abbey that he loved, he rediscovered the ancient practices of contemplation.

"We didn't do contemplation back then," Luke explained. "The Trappists were under the influence of those who had condemned Madame Guyon and her teaching that Christians were supposed to go seeking a certain sort of religious experience. 'No experience,' we used to teach here. It was asceticism we focused on—asceticism, penance, and work. But Thomas Keating changed all of that. He brought us back to our truer roots.

"Upon returning home, the first thing that Father Thomas did with his novice students was to take away their holy cards, their medals, and their icons and other images," Luke explained. "He wasn't instituting a new set of laws, and he certainly wasn't pronouncing these things wrong, but he asked the men to seek God in a new way."

This was a radical change for the monks in those days, but it wasn't a new idea. Cardinal Newman once said, "This I know full well . . . that the Catholic Church allows no image of any sort, material or immaterial, no dogmatic symbol, no rite, no sacrament, no Saint, not even the Blessed Virgin herself, to come between the soul and its Creator. It is face to face, *solus cum solo*, in all matters between man and his God."[2]

Merton, for his part, shows this change in spirit by 1958. More than sixteen years after first joining the Trappists and long after *The Seven Storey Mountain* had made him the most famous monk of the twentieth century, Merton suddenly saw the world as it really was. In his earlier writings, Merton wrote enthusiastically about how monks are men who have rejected the world so as to embrace it more profoundly, in prayer. A monk is a man who turns away from the world of people and chaos and things, in order to dedicate himself to pray for the salvation of that same world. That was his understanding for the first decade and a half in the monastery.

But on March 18, 1958, Merton was in Louisville on a rare visit to the city. Walking down the street toward the busy corner of Fourth Avenue and Walnut, he suddenly realized that he loved all of the people before him.

> I was suddenly overwhelmed with the realization that I loved all these people, that they were mine and I theirs, that we could not be alien to one another even though we were total strangers. It was like waking from a dream of separateness, of spurious self-isolation in a special world, the world of renunciation and supposed holiness. The whole illusion of a separate holy existence is a dream. Not that I question the reality of my vocation, or of my monastic life: but the conception of "separation from the world" that we have in the monastery too easily presents itself as a complete illusion . . . We are in the same world as everybody else, the world of the bomb, the world of race hatred, the world of technology, the world of mass media, big business, revolution, and all the rest . . . This

119

sense of liberation from an illusory difference was such a relief and such a joy to me that I almost laughed out loud . . . To think that for sixteen or seventeen years I have been taking seriously this pure illusion that is implicit in so much of our monastic thinking . . . I have the immense joy of being man, a member of a race in which God Himself became incarnate. As if the sorrows and stupidities of the human condition could overwhelm me, now I realize what we all are. And if only everybody could realize this! But it cannot be explained. There is no way of telling people that they are all walking around shining like the sun.[3]

"Now, I understand the problems of ambition," I said to Father Matthew one morning. "But can we return to the idea of undoing my originality?"

"Of course."

"Why is it bad to be original?"

"You are unique, but it shouldn't be your ambition. Your good parents probably taught you to become an original, to stand out, be someone special?"

"Yes, I'm sure that that's right," I told him.

"Well, for a monk, there is a different way to success."

"What's that?"

"Imitation—the opposite of being an original. St. Paul wrote that true freedom comes when we see ourselves become reflections of Christ. And Benedict bases most of his Rule on this premise: that human happiness comes when we are not original, but copies," Matthew explained.

"My mother won't like that," I joked. "She told me to stand out, to be special."

"A monk wants to strive for the opposite of originality. A monk will commit to blending in, to becoming almost lost in the sea of white robes."

8

LIFE AND DEATH

soul
"place right hand on forehead, then raise it, looking upwards"

—*A Dictionary of the Cistercian Sign Language*

Brother Leonard was 102 when he died on Christmas Eve, 2007.

On December 23, after a trip to the bathroom and laughing at a joke made by a nurse in the infirmary at St. Joseph's Abbey, he lay down on his bed and stopped breathing. His body was completely blanched and the nurse quickly called for the abbot. That's what you do in a monastery when one of the elderly brothers has died: you call for the abbot. He came very quickly, rushing to the bedside of a monk who was loved dearly by all.

Everyone knew that Brother Leonard was going to die soon. He was 102, after all, and ill. He had been living in the infirmary for several years by this point in time because it's easier to care for the older and ailing monks when they reside where the nurses come and go, and where the other brothers are always helping out.

When the abbot arrived at the infirmary, he walked slowly over to the bed in which Brother Leonard's body quietly lay. The death of a brother is a time of the utmost decorum and reverence. The abbot stood in silence about to begin the customary prayers for the dead—when Leonard suddenly popped up in bed and looked him straight in the eyes.

"A shocking moment," Father Luke said, "to say the least!"

Leonard was then conscious for another full day, talking off and on with the abbot, his brothers, and the nurses.

"Lenny," as his brothers called him, "was clearly preparing to die," Father Luke explained. And he would go to God the following day after saying goodbye, after having a private moment with each of his brothers.

Brother Lenny was known as one who loved others completely and unreservedly, and his brothers took care of him in a special way in those last days and hours. According to Trappist tradition, at least one brother was always at his bedside during the final hours. And after death had come, there were two brothers who "watched" at the side of the body every moment before it was buried in the monastery burial ground. This means that they were there, awake, contemplating the resurrection of Christ and praying for Lenny to be taken into the divine embrace. They recited the psalms and intoned other prayers, often by the dim candlelight of a mostly dark abbey church. Cardinal John Henry Newman once said, "We are not simply to believe, but to watch;

not simply to love, but to watch; not simply to obey, but to watch." To watch is "to be detached from what is present, and to live in what is unseen; to live in the thought of Christ as he came once, and as he will come again; to desire his second coming."[1]

———— ∞∞ ————

Not every monk dies as easily as Brother Leonard died, but their lives often seem to end in lovely ways. And a monastery seems an appropriate place to contemplate the meaning of life and death.

Years ago, en route on one of my visits to the monastery in Georgia, I stopped at a remote gas station not far from the abbey. Of the delicacies on sale near the counter was Cracklin Brand porkskins made in nearby East Point, Georgia. For ninety-nine cents I could have purchased something advertised boldly on the packaging as "Fried Out Pork Fat with Attached Skin." That was a new one for me. I picked up a diet Coke instead. *My last one of these for a while*, I thought to myself, and then drove the remaining miles to the abbey gates. On an earlier occasion—one of my first monastery visits—I remember stopping at a steakhouse by the highway and gorging myself, complete with hot fudge sundae for dessert, thinking that it was the last good meal I'd eat for a while. Was I ever wrong! Monastery food consistently reminds me of how easy it is to be vegetarian and eat well—if someone else is doing all of the preparation and cooking!

If you arrive at an abbey on a Friday afternoon in the summertime, chances are the brother at the welcome desk in the retreat house will be able to tell you the score of the big baseball game. He may be watching it on his computer. On this occasion in Georgia, I found a note: "Welcome, Jon.

This is your key. Your room is upstairs, down on the left. If you need anything, let me know." It was signed by the retreat director, one of the monks, and a small envelope contained my key.

"Thanks," I said with a wave, looking at the monk sitting inside the office at the entrance to the retreat house. *Was he the one who wrote the note?*

A few moments later, I dropped my bag on the floor and collapsed on the bed. A crucifix was fixed on the wall above me, but not the bloody kind. *It could hit me in the head while I'm sleeping*, I thought. So I sat up. On a small desk sat a small clock and an old lamp with a tan shade. There were three lonely hangers in the closet and I used them all, wishing for a couple more.

In a retreat house, everything is orderly and clean, and excessively simple. The blankets never have stains, for instance, like the ones occasionally seen in shelters, nursing homes, or even low-cost hotels, but they may show signs of wear. I once ripped one easily by trying to pull it up to my chin on a cold night.

My window was about five feet off the floor, away from all furniture, and designed not for looking through but simply for daylight. Sitting on the edge of the bed I could only see blue sky and treetops out the window. But when standing right in front of it, I could see a lake in the distance. I could also see the monastery burial ground just below me: simple white crosses, each identical to the next except for the grayness of the limestone, which seemed to indicate age. The crosses follow a geometric symmetry: five horizontal rows, eight across per row. *A good place to contemplate death*, I thought to myself.

Only two of the rows appear to be complete, however: two and four. Row one has an available eighth place to be filled on one end; row five has five available spots; and row three, one space to be filled between crosses six and eight. All of this seems odd to me. *Do they reserve certain spots for certain guys?*

In row three, for instance, a certain Brother Vincent and Brother Peter are separated by one empty space between them. I wonder why. *Did Vincent and Peter have some sort of feud? Who will fit between them someday?*

I asked Father Peter about it later that afternoon. "Does he already know that is his designated spot—whichever monk will be buried between Vincent and Peter?"

"Yes, probably he does," he said. "A monk may request a specific burial place, and sometimes he will ask to be buried beside a friend."

Most Christian theologians tell us we did not exist before we were born. There is no reservoir of available immortal souls, in heaven, awaiting their proper appointment by God. A human soul is not created by the child's parents, and it is uncreated altogether until the moment that a child is conceived.

But from that moment on, the unity between soul and body is a profound one, the soul giving form to the body (according to the Council of Vienne in 1312), and the two parts together making one person. Only at death are they separated, and then, only for a time.

I recounted all of this to Brother Samuel one morning, explaining that I was studying the meaning of Christian birth and death. We were sitting in the receiving room where guests are able to meet with one of the monks. I had been invited to lunch and the smell of sweet potato fries was wafting over our heads as we talked.

Samuel nodded. "Yes, I think there is something to that. I'm not a theologian, though, and I don't think a great deal about those distinctions," he said.

"Do you think about death?" I asked him.

"Of course I do. Don't you?"

I do, but not very fruitfully, I thought to myself. "Yes," I replied.

"I know that I understand it more as my body breaks down." Brother Samuel was eighty at this time—a robust eighty, but an octogenarian nonetheless. "I am enjoying the changes in my mind, for instance. I don't remember what I once did, and that's fine with me. I feel like I'm surrendering a bit, and as I do, love fills me in those spaces where, perhaps, used to be my confidence in my own capacities."

"That is beautiful," I told him. But again, it was one of those frustrating moments. *How practical is that?* I thought to myself. "Do you think that your experience is common?" I asked.

"I'm not sure. But I *am* sure that there is love and understanding inside of each person. From the moment you

Monastic Burial Practices

Today many non-Catholics are looking to the monastic orders for guidance on Christian burial practices. Concerned with the ways that profit and legislation have entered into the ways that we prepare and handle burying our loved ones, some people have created a small renaissance of ancient Christian practices in this area. Monastic burial practices include loved ones washing the body before calling the funeral home, burial on private land rather than in cemeteries (allowed in some states), burial without embalming (also allowed in only certain states), and the use of simple wooden caskets. In fact, the Trappist abbey in Iowa offers wooden, monastic-style caskets and urns to be preordered, handmade, and held on their premises awaiting a death in the family.

began life as a created cell, your body and soul have traveled together. Sometimes—especially when you're younger—the body crowds out the soul, and other times—maybe most often when you're older like me—the soul becomes more obvious."

He continued, "What I know of death is that it is beautiful; even when it's painful and horrible, there's a dark sort of beauty. And you have to begin abandoning yourself to God in order to know it."

The monastic life is so ancient and full of tradition that it gives off the wrong impression sometimes. When I look at the brothers in their long gowns I sometimes imagine a static and unchanging life. I've reassured myself in crazy times by thinking, *at least some things, like the monks, always remain constant*. But even they don't. Monastic life changes and evolves; even the traditions change.

A brother can easily look sad by outward appearance. The cowl breeds anonymity, and status becomes irrelevant. They tend not to be concerned with either outward appearance or, for that matter, others' perceptions of them. On several occasions I have found myself wondering, *Why doesn't he seem happier to see me?* only to remember this.

Maybe only a contemplative can understand death before it happens. The promise of a contemplative life is not passion so much as it is dispassion. Its primary personal expression, contemplative prayer, aims at interior silence and stillness. Its primary corporate expression, chanting the daily liturgical hours of prayer, aims at achieving equanimity of soul. And so Trappist monks are very rarely Elijah or John the Baptist types. They are not wild, untamed, sensuous. Instead, contemplative monks trace their roots through northern

European monasticism: they are unmoved, most often dispassionate. Even those guys who have "fallen in love," spending hours and hours in the church, do it really quietly.

This may be one of the reasons why monks tend to live longer than the rest of us.

Researchers in The Netherlands, for instance, studied 1,523 contemplative monks from 1900–1994 and discovered that the monks' mortality rate was consistently lower than men in the general population.[2] It is ironic that men who consciously prepare themselves to die, embracing it as another doorway of life, actually take longer to get there.

One of John Cassian's great affections was for his *cella* or cell—his little room in the community. As an abbot, he taught his monks to love this tiny enclosed space, like a bird loves its nest or a worm its hole. He learned from his time in the Egyptian desert the saying, "The cell will teach you all you need to know."

"This is the greatest of all understandings," Basil once told me. "To stop fleeing. Stop running. Stop trying to entertain yourself, or escape yourself. To love your cell means to love who you are when you are alone with God. Contemplation— or any real and authentic response to the Father—cannot begin until it begins there."

The days of a monk beating himself up in private ascesis (rigorous self-denial) are long gone. There may still be the occasional hair shirt and scapular, but that's about it. Don't look for any dark *Da Vinci Code* scenes in the private cells of today's monasteries. You won't find them. Occasionally a Trappist will receive permission to live as a semi-hermit on the property for a time. If that happens, his cell becomes even more important to him, and he spends as much time there as he can, while still taking most meals together with his brothers and praying at least the major "hours" of the day, at the monastery. Even these semi-hermits (Thomas Merton was one) remain in meaningful ways members of their communities.

If there is one thing that the repetitive, daily, God-directed life of a contemplative community reminds me, it is this: every aspect of my life is temporary, and that's good. I mustn't fool myself that I will endure as I am, or that I can build impenetrable walls around myself. Nor should I want to. "Advertisers will tell you differently," Father Samuel told me, "but the monastic life shows Christians, even the very involved ones, that things like worship and liturgy, and morality and virtue, must be transcended on a personal level, in communion with God."

"And there's some sort of connection between this private communion and understanding your mortality?" I asked.

"Yes."

Dom Basil once wrote in an e-mail about the death and funeral of his friend, Jim, "The little wooden chest is beautifully crafted. The monks of New Melleray make coffins and boxes for cremains from the hardwood trees harvested from their forest, the largest privately owned forest in Iowa. This particular box was made with particular care and love for it was for one of our own . . . Jim. We had survived the 'horrors' of the novitiate together and sailed on through over fifty happy, blessed and privileged years, always trying to say 'yes' to whatever the Lord asked—many things that were not in the postulants' guide. And now he was gone on ahead. And it hurts."

Basil went on: "I do believe in the resurrection of the body, but it still hurts . . . After an abbatial Mass, we will carry

129

Jim's ashes solemnly down the cloisters to bury them in our community cemetery. The small bell will toll, bespeaking our sorrow and loss. But at the same time the great bell will ring out in full peal, an Easter proclamation: Christ is risen; he is truly risen. And Jim will rise again."

Two years after Basil wrote these words about his monk friend, I was present when the monks buried Basil. He died in 2005 from injuries suffered in a car accident. A pick-up truck slammed into the side of the car that Basil was driving only a few miles from the monastery.

The first thing I remember hearing after Basil's funeral and burial, as I walked into the abbey library, was the resounding popping of opening beer and soda cans. Walking from the yard outside where we had just buried him, through the cloisters, I crossed the threshold into the library where refreshments had been set up. I wasn't the first person in the room, and many of those before me had already begun to celebrate. What a beautiful sound that popping was! The food and drink was as abundant as Basil's overflowing life had been. The bins of beer and soda cans on ice went quickly as we toasted and celebrated a lovely man.

Few liturgical services are more beautiful in a Trappist monastery than Compline at the end of the day. It seems to symbolize all of monastic life, including the awareness of death. The word Compline comes from a Latin word (*completorium*) which means "to complete" or "to close." The Compline prayers and ritual complete the Christian day. They are also said before it is time to retire for the night.

Since the monks of Basil's old monastery in Georgia allow the retreatants to sit in the choir stalls right beside them, we pray right alongside fresh-faced novices and wizened veterans that sometimes look like they've stepped out of *The Name of the Rose*, chanting the same words.

Father Anthony once told me, "Compline completes each day by recognizing we are creatures only, creatures before our Creator. When you have truly 'made the Lord your refuge,' as we pray in Psalm 91, you are at home whether you are awake, asleep, alive, or dead."

The sanctuary is almost completely darkened. The only light comes from a few candles that are inexplicably flickering in the middle of an immense, concrete church. In the darkness, the chanted psalms and prayers seem to bounce off the walls even more than usual.

Each monk, and others of us who are participating, processes past the abbot in a single-file line, slowly walking and watching the robe or feet of the person ahead of us. The abbot gently sprinkles water on each person's head. Then we continue our prayer and mindfulness from the sanctuary to our cells. It is at moments such as these that I am prepared to call my room my cella.

The only audible sound in the church at the end of Compline is the shuffling of feet on the stone floor as we walk silently past the abbot and from the abbot to our cells and to sleep. It reminds me of the communion of saints on every occasion that I hear it.

The nursery rhyme, "Now I lay me down to sleep"—which honestly, if you actually listen to the words, seems so inappropriate for young children—is necessary for grown-up faith and is the essential message of Compline: "Now I lay me down to sleep, I pray the Lord my soul to keep. If I should die before I wake, I pray the Lord my soul to take." Even better, a few lines from poet Jane Kenyon:

Let it come, as it will, and don't
be afraid. God does not leave us
comfortless, so let evening come.

—"Let Evening Come"

One of the characters in a Muriel Spark novel says, "If I had my life over again I should form the habit of nightly composing myself to thoughts of death . . . Death, when it approaches, ought not to take one by surprise. It should be part of the full expectancy of life. Without an ever-present sense of death life is inspid."[3]

The monks have taught me to see it that way too. When it comes, I hope to live up to their wisdom.

"Do you think about your death?" I asked Father Luke one morning.

"I do," he smiled.

"And . . . what do you think about?"

"God has taken care of me all my life and he'll take care of me now, in death."

"But what about a slow death? Going quickly is one thing, but what about the slow falling-apart of the body? You are in your late seventies, right? You must have thought about that?"

"Even illness can be an *adventure*. *Death* is an adventure."

9

Be Home. Love.

to thank
"bring hand to mouth as though about to kiss it; or kiss tips
of right fingers"

—A Dictionary of the Cistercian Sign Language

By the winter of 2008 I am separated from my wife. To
be honest, I don't exactly know why our marriage is
ending, and that's what makes it so difficult. She has
become convinced that she can't live with me anymore. In
the middle of all of this, I visit Father Luke at the monastery
in early February. On a rainy, foggy winter morning, I drive
down from Vermont to see him.

This is the third visit to see Father Luke since I've learned
a new way of driving down. I take back roads that travel
through the serene hills of western Massachusetts. After exit-
ing off of Interstate 91 South and heading east onto Route 2,

I breathe deeply. *I'll be there, soon.* Driving on Route 2 for fifteen minutes or so, I finally see the exit that will take me in a southward direction again. I slow down just enough to take the right hand turn and then slide onto Route 122 South. The fog is becoming thicker and I can hardly see, but I'm in a hurry to get there. I'm always in a hurry to get there, wherever there is.

That lovely lake is coming up on the right, I say out loud to no one, and just as the dark and icy waters come into my peripheral vision a large white owl suddenly appears as well, precisely at the height of my car antenna and almost as close, directly in front of the car, not exactly flying—more like floating—from the lakeside to the woods on my left. I slam on the brakes out of shock more than anything else, and the car spins once around, settling almost perfectly on

Tools in the Spiritual Workshop

My favorite chapter in the Rule of St. Benedict is the fourth. In it, Benedict prioritizes the good works of a monk, and also, how to do them—in other words, what tools to use to accomplish the tasks. Many of the good works he lists are of the obvious sort—Ten Commandments kind of stuff. But there are some surprises. Monks are asked, for instance, to "bury the dead" and "to dread hell," both of which have much to do with the medieval mindset. But there are others that uniquely aim a monk at virtue. For example, "not to cherish an opportunity for displaying one's anger" and "not to give the kiss of peace insincerely." A few of the injunctions reflect values that are still kept in monasteries, but in very few other places: "to revere the elders," "to pray for one's enemies in the love of Christ," and "after a quarrel to make peace with the other before sunset." Finally, I love the language that emphasizes the unity of the human person that once existed, when one was believed to respond to God with body/soul (without distinction) at once. Benedict reminds the monks: "to fall often to prayer," as in, literally, to one's knees.[1]

the right-hand side of the road beside the lake. *Oh, God!* is all that I can find to say, my heart pounding.

Sitting there on the side of the road for five minutes or so, I finally put the car back into gear and drive the remaining half hour down to the abbey.

My wife and the owl are both on my mind when I arrive, but for some reason I can't talk about either of them. I know all about the tradition of spiritual direction. I have good friends to whom I tell almost everything, and I regularly offer a formal confession to my parish priest, but I've never had a real spiritual director. Father Luke has almost been that for me, but not entirely. And I definitely haven't told him everything. *I'm not ready*, I think to myself.

We sit down in our customary chairs by the windows. *It is still foggy*, I think, looking out over the valley toward Worcester. *I can't even see my car from here.*

I didn't realize that I had spoken out loud. "Yes, it has been like that all morning," Luke said.

"Do you ever wonder, Father Luke, what is the purpose of all of the spiritual exercises we do?" I asked him.

He looked a bit askance at me.

"I mean, what's the purpose of it all?"

"That's not your usual sort of question," he said.

I waited. "You don't look at the sun directly, Jon," he added.

"What does that mean?" I asked.

"If you mean: 'Do I believe that there is a God and that I am here to know him,' then yes, I never doubt it for a moment."

Luke is talking firmly today, I thought.

"I do so much, I try so hard . . ." I began.

135

"So what. What does that matter?"

"What do you mean: what does that matter? What else is there?"

"Plenty."

"You don't make yourself spiritual," Luke said. "And you are thinking mostly about yourself if you are self-consciously trying for that. Prayer and *lectio* and going to church—those are duties, not spiritualities. You don't chart your own course to holiness."

"Then what do I do?" I say, with more pleading in my heart than he can possibly imagine.

"You can keep loving."

Sitting with Father Luke on that foggy February morning, my mind wandered back to a sunnier time when he and I were walking from the retreat house to a hillside overlooking the grassy valley on a May afternoon. We had settled into some wooden folding chairs and tilted our faces up to the sun. The natural heat felt really good on my dry, white, winter face. That was before we knew each other very well.

I snapped back into the moment. "I don't think I've ever heard you use the words *spiritual* or *spirituality* until just a minute ago," I said to him.

"Is that right? Well, I suppose that they are not very useful words. They mean too many things to too many people."

"What do they mean to you?" I asked.

"Not much, to be honest with you."

"Really?"

"Yes. I'm not trying to be spiritual."

I was startled by this. "Why not?"

"It's the wrong goal and the wrong path, both.

"The words of spirituality often don't ring true for me. They are always so comforting. But knowing God intimately isn't always a comfort. Anyone who has spent long periods of time listening for God's voice knows that the experience is not often warm or cozy or even inviting. It can be profoundly unsettling," he warned.

I knew what he meant, but recent troubles had sidetracked me. I go through times when the words and sentences of spiritual-talk begin to turn me off. "I am *deep* listening to you," a friend once pronounced as I told her a fairly painful story about something that was happening in my life. Her sympathetic expression only made it sound worse. *Just listen, don't* deep *listen!* I felt inside.

<hr />

There is an old Italian proverb: *L'abito non fa il monaco.* "The habit does not make the monk." Often paraphrased to mean something akin to "You can't judge a book by its cover"—the meaning is actually in the reverse: Your behavior—as in, a monk wearing the right clothing—doesn't always indicate who you are.

Many of us outside the cloister spend far too much time working on being spiritual. We attend retreats, we buy books, we buy CDs, we learn new techniques, repeat mantras, do a little yoga, sometimes with the aim more of being spiritual than of knowing God. Monks show how "being spiritual" is almost entirely beside the point of the Christian life.

My evangelical Christian grandparents used to tell me not to be religious. We were independent Baptists because denominations were not to be trusted. Denominations were, like presbyters and bishops and other institutions, believed to be unnecessary impediments between you and God. This is one of my grandparents' teachings that I rejected long ago.

I love religion and many of its trappings. I love what the Catholics call "sacramentals"—those ordinary physical things that we sanctify through use in making the world holy. Water, made holy water; minerals and herbs, made incense; round stones, made into prayer beads. And I love the liturgy, the tradition, the prayers. I don't share my grandparents' desire for the end of religion, but I'm beginning to embrace the possible end of spirituality.

Where does Jesus say to his disciples, "Be spiritual for I am spiritual"?

"Don't make prayer or service or study or whatever, something you set out to do like a task. Love your neighbor to the point of giving yourself up to him. Then, see what God would have you do next," Dom Basil once said to me.

The first of the desert monks, St. Anthony of Egypt, said, "He prays best who doesn't know that he is praying." Some have taken this to mean that you should "lose yourself" in prayer, losing all track of time and place, like a trance. But I don't think that's it. Not being spiritual means forgetting about the trappings of your prayer; when you are really doing it you will know.

We aren't supposed to try and find spiritual experiences. We aren't supposed to measure our success by how we feel or what we've done. We are meant to become our true selves in Christ, which for many people may mean avoiding spirituality altogether.

Each person discovers how he is an expression—a unique copy, as Father Matthew would paradoxically put it—of Christ in the world, with God's help. And sometimes, with God's help, we don't discover it or we feel lost in the midst of trying. That's okay. That's better than being spiritual. It is when we all seem alike that we have the clearest indication that it's spirituality we're tracking with, rather than Christ.

———— ⌘ ————

I felt my jaw tighten.

I had been stuck in traffic for nearly five hours, having traveled only twenty miles through downtown Boston in the worst blizzard in years. I left my office south of the city at noon, imagining that I'd be home before the worst of the storm hit. But by now the sun had set and the snow was screaming sideways in the glow of the overhead highway lamps. This was one of those days when every employer in Boston told their employees to go home early, so all the commuters were trying to get home at the same time. I was so frustrated that I was about to burst out of my skin.

At one point, I and other motorists were standing outside of our cars on an overpass for twenty full minutes with nowhere to go, brushing wet snow off our rear windows, scraping away ice that was beginning to place a thick frosting underneath our wiper blades. We stood around and used our cell phones. I called a friend in Florida who said that the sun was shining and it was about eighty degrees. "I'm sorry that I have to go, but I have to get my shorts on and change my shoes; we're having a pool party," he said. He was serious.

Soon after the overpass, as I crept along at four miles per hour, I was cut off by a young woman in another car. It was then that I really began to clench my teeth. *There's nowhere to go! Why are you cutting me off!* I screamed to my windshield. I had just about had it.

I was only a quarter of a mile farther along the road ten minutes later. A lane of traffic to my right was merging with mine. I quickly decided that I was going to be one of *those* people too. I was going to cut someone off if it meant that I could move ahead even five or six car-lengths. I gave the gas pedal a quick pump, merged into the lane, and then abruptly picked a spot where I could sneak safely in to the left. The road was slick and the car behind me almost slid into the back of mine.

The young man in the car behind me was clearly upset, making his feelings known in a variety of ways familiar to any commuter. He gestured and he screamed, even putting his window down in order to add emphasis. My first instinct was to be demonstrative in return, even though there are other times when I might shrink away from such a situation entirely. I don't really like confrontation; it's just that traffic brings out the worst in me.

He was still yelling three minutes later, and I was beginning to feel regret. I remembered something I once saw a monk do while talking about having to forgive a horrible wrong. It was an old gesture of Cistercian sign language. I looked in my rearview mirror at the younger man, put my palms together in a gesture of blessing, and mouthed the words, "I'm sorry."

The young man's reaction shocked me. His eyes widened and he paused. A moment later, he gave me a thumbs up sign with a small grin. We ended up waving to each other about a half hour later as the traffic finally broke apart and we sped away.

I am beginning to see the effects of monastic life in my own secular life. For one thing, I'm beginning to stop using that term, *secular life*. My life is *not* secular. As Dom Basil would say, "Where is God if God is all around you?" God is in my heart, my intentions, my hands and feet, and my loves are all pointed in the right directions, even though I of course fail all the time. As I've heard Desmond Tutu remark, "Nothing is secular except sin."

"How do you know when you have been transformed by grace?" I ask Father Luke on a February afternoon.

He gives me a funny look and I imagine that I know the reason why.

"I know . . . it's a crazy question, or an impossible one, but from your perspective, having been a monk for the last 60 years: Do you feel transformed by grace? Do you, can you, know it?"

He sighs and shakes his head. "No, I don't believe that you can know that.

"All that you can know is whether God has you in the darkness or the light," he continues. "You cannot know grace just like you cannot earn it. You cannot will yourself to an intimate relationship with God that feels warm and secure any more than you can will your partner to love you forever. Sure, you can try. We all try. But your trying won't do much of anything. 'God rewards those who try,' right, that's what we say? Ha!" and he gave a throaty laugh. "Try all you can, but asking and waiting is what's really required."

The Christian mystical tradition—from Augustine to John Wesley to Henri Nouwen—is very clear on this point: You can't know. All of the spirituality in the world doesn't change the fact that you have to trust and hope and pay attention to where God has you at all times. The meaning of life for the contemplative monk is to rest in God knowing that you don't know the meaning of life. Thomas Merton says, "What is the use of praying if at the very moment of prayer, we have so little confidence in God that we are busy planning our own kind of answer to our prayer?"[2] Wait. Listen. Wait some more.

———— ✼ ————

Many of the best-selling books today are written by critics of religion, rather than by devotees. An entire industry has popped up around people like Richard Dawkins (*The God Delusion*), Christopher Hitchens (*Why God Is Not Great*), and Sam Harris (*Letter to a Christian Nation*). The anti-religion book has become the hottest subgenre in the religion section at your local bookstore. Surely, the spin-off products are coming soon. Will there soon be replacement kitsch for those who were once religious but are no longer? Huggable Darwin plush toys (I've actually seen these), human brains on silver pendants, icon cards of Nietszche or maybe even of Dawkins, Hitchens, and Harris?

"I read that book," Father Luke tells me when I begin asking about the latest best-seller. I'm always amazed at how current he is on books and current events. "A very smart man, but he's frustrated," Luke reflects.

Proud atheists are the new champions of the latest round of religion debunking, or better put, faith debunking. If you still have some sort of faith in God, you are supposed to feel somehow foolish, or even dangerous, to the rest of the world. The new atheists believe that faith is what caused 9/11; faith is what has caused wars, conflict, and prejudice throughout history. And of course, they are right, but only in part. They only tell part of the story of faith and its effects.

The crowd who eats up this antireligion stuff recently became all excited about revelations that Mother Teresa of Calcutta had serious doubts in her faith over the last fifty years of her life. The story hit the cover of *Time* magazine, and a couple of weeks later in *Newsweek*, Hitchens (not to be outdone) wrote, "The Church should have had the elementary decency to let the earth lie lightly on this troubled and miserable lady, and not to invoke her long anguish to recruit the credulous to a blind faith in which she herself long ceased to believe."[3]

But Mother Teresa's letters don't tell of a loss of faith or the foolishness of faith, just like when a monk talks with me of spending months of years "in darkness" he is not talking about a lack of sunlight or a lack of faith. He's simply talking about where God wants him, where God has put him for the time being.

There is a story from the Indian scriptures, the Upanishads, in which a father teaches his son about God as Spirit. The father asks the son to pour salt into a glass of water and allow the salt to dissolve. "Taste the water from that side of the glass," he tells the boy. "Now, taste the water from the other side." The boy admits to tasting the salt even though he cannot see it, and the father explains that this is how it is with God.

Ask a person of faith, with a commitment to faith, "How often do you have doubts?" and you will hear, "All of the time!" Overcoming intellectual doubts and doing extra spirituality exercises isn't what it's all about, and a loss of faith is not an end. It's an aridity like needing water in the desert. And since faith is a gift, aridity is God's doing, not your lack of trying. Try all you want—it's almost beside the point.

Mother Teresa's doubting began long before she became "Mother" anything, and even before she established the Missionaries of Charity in India. Early on, she recognized how her union with God in Christ would often be dark. "Do not think that my spiritual life is strewn with roses—that is the flower which I hardly ever find on my way. Quite the contrary, I have more often as my companion, 'darkness.' And when the night becomes very thick—and it seems to me as if I will end up in hell—then I simply offer myself to Jesus," she wrote to her confessor back home, as a young woman. And, she says over and over in other letters to her confessors, she rarely heard an answer from Jesus when she would offer herself and ask for guidance in these matters.

"Does that sound familiar to you?" I asked Father Luke, "to your own experience?"

"Yes, and the world seems to divide between those who can see this and those who cannot. Nevertheless, God wants us all," Father Luke replied, "and God's grace doesn't reach us all in the same way or at the same time."

"Faith will never make sense to people like Dawkins and Hitchens until it grabs them by the chin," Luke tells me. I think he's mixing his metaphors again, but I get it.

Mystics describe personal faith in terms that can never work in discussions of what is logical and illogical, true and false, verifiable or not. The faith of Mother Teresa was in the ground of her being; it was a mystical union. This being rests and this union takes place in ways that are beyond good explanation. Sometimes only metaphors will suffice; the source of our being and union is like a river running quietly below the surface of the earth—churches drink from this river, and so do people of faith of all kinds, but some people travel it intimately, and they sometimes do so in darkness.

I'm beginning to accept things, to listen, to be still. I started out on this monastic journey with a lot of earnestness and lists of things to learn. I've done a lot. I've tried really hard. But each time I stop trying so hard and listen more, I feel like I'm at home. I can be a thousand miles away from the nearest monastery, and like a bat in the woods, I know where I'm going.

"I feel sorry for the atheist who says, 'Prove it to me. I can't see it,' " said Father Luke to me one afternoon.

"You mean, because of what he's missing?" I ask.

"He's a materialist. The atheist and the skeptic are stuck in a carapace of materiality. God is beyond. The spirit life is real, if you will live it."

For so many reasons, faith is a dark road. That doesn't make it wrong or foolish, but it can be dry and without much in the way of clear consolation. This is why Trappist monks will tell you to stop bothering with trying to be spiritual.

Father Luke explained, "And then, of course, as St. John of the Cross was quick to point out, if you feel in the darkness about spiritual things it can sometimes mean that God has actually drawn near to you. How did he put it? A wet log—that's what we are like—a wet log and God's flame is underneath us trying to make some sort of dent. Sometimes God has very little noticeable effect on us. It takes time. That's why we're patient."

Some of my friendships with monks were relationships that began because of Basil Pennington's influence, and then deepened after his death. In some cases, Basil's friends became my friends, as I love to talk about him and listen to the experiences others had with him.

"You still love him," Father Luke reminded me one afternoon. "He's gone, but he's still here, and he's loving you. Boy, could Basil love!" he concluded with a smile and a glance out the window.

Real love is so illusive that reality TV dating shows, Internet dating, explicit YouTube videos, and celebrity voyeurism have all burst like bulls out of the tunnel. "There's clearly enormous potential, and a desperate market, for real love in the world," Father Luke said to me that afternoon, sounding almost businesslike. "There's a hugely needy market out there for what we're offering," he said.

"Why do you love someone? *How* do you love them?" I asked.

"Love, real love, is far more rare than violence. And real love is more personally dangerous to us than violence."

"I don't understand."

"You suffer it," he told me, "which means that becoming open so as to truly love leads to new depth of life, and that depth includes pain."

"Yes, I know what you mean," I said.

The happy-go-lucky-I-love-everyone sort of blather makes no sense in the context of monastic life and teaching. To love everyone can sometimes amount to truly loving no one. Jesus and St. Benedict both said that to love is to make yourself personally vulnerable. Hospitality, for instance, does not simply mean a bowl of soup and a place to sleep, but also an open heart. To care for the stranger is to be open to him, to be willing to be wounded by him. These are, again, much harder words to live than to say.

I remember the moment that my first child was born. I don't believe that I knew the meaning of love until that moment when she emerged from the womb literally into my waiting arms. It was at that precise moment in April 1993 that I knew for the first time what it felt like to have my heart broken. I loved like I never had before, but I was also in pain, woundedly open. I wouldn't trade the experience for the world—but I've also never really duplicated it.

"*That's* the kind of love, real self-giving love, that we all are supposed to participate in all of the time. We fall short," Luke concluded.

"So how do we do better?" I asked him.

"Don't try harder. Find your home with God, and remain there."

———⟨≈⟩———

Father Ambrose once told me the following story as we talked in the retreat house in Georgia:

"Years ago, the philosopher Aldous Huxley was giving a talk on cosmology to a large audience somewhere. When he was done talking, during the question and answer period that followed, an elderly woman stood up.

'Dr. Huxley, that was all very interesting, but you've gotten it wrong. The world is actually flat.'

'That's one theory,' Huxley replied slowly in his reserved manner. 'What, Madam, would you say holds this flat world up?'

'It rests on the back of a turtle,' the woman replied.

A bemused Huxley said, 'And so, Madam, what then does the turtle stand upon . . . ?'

'On the back of another turtle.'

'And . . . what does that turtle stand upon . . . ?'

'Yes, yes, yes,' the elderly woman interrupted, 'I know where you're going, Mr. Huxley. Don't bother yourself. The answer is: It's turtles all the way down.'"

Ambrose laughed out loud at his own story, and he added, "This is the only real Christian truth: it doesn't make a whole lot of sense, but it's love all the way down."

Postscript

Ambrose wrote: "After more than fifty years in the monastery, the questions seem even greater, and the answers, mostly more tentative. Life, I've discovered, is fascinating but coquettish. Still, my fascination tempts me and draws me on like the rueful, ever hopeful, lover, longing to know and despairing to understand my Beloved more deeply."

I carried that letter around with me for several years, referring to it often.

It seems to me that my life has gone through four stages thus far. These steps have marked my progress as a boy growing into a man and as a child with faith into a mature adult. Stage one I would call the received tradition. I received the Word and what it said; I did not challenge it. Simultaneously, I was the son of good parents and I was taught, as hopefully all kids are, to obey mommy and daddy, to do what they say. For the most part, I did that and that was good. Some people probably remain at this sort of stage for their entire lives and it's not necessarily wrong.

But I would call stage two the rebel stage. Some wise person once told me that spiritual maturity is impossible for a man without at some point rebelling against his father. This was true for me. My rebellions were relatively mild compared to those of many of my friends, but still, I rebelled in important ways. I challenged that earlier Word, calling it nonsense at times, and I left the church, wandering around through other traditions and figuring that I knew what was right. Again, some people probably remain at this stage for their entire lives.

Stage three is the one that I'm mostly in right now. I would call it the spirituality stage, when practice and ritual have become vital in my life, and I have rewoven connections to the religion of my youth as well as to some religious practices that were never a part of my youth but that I've decided are important. The patchwork I've been creating makes a different pattern from the received tradition of my first stage, and, I think, it makes a better one.

But stage four is where I am being led by the monks. It is where they are right now and where I try to be when I can. At this stage in my life, I am moving beyond spirituality and its program of self by becoming more contemplative. The questions and issues of my earlier rebellions are not answered any more than they were when I was in stage two, but I also don't fight them as much anymore. The answer to many of the questions of life comes when the questions themselves fade away as less important. In this contemplative stage of life, I also find myself feeling more profoundly connected to those around me: I want to be near strangers and I want more connections with those who are already friends.

I've been blessed by the monks in my life and they remind me that when I'm dead, my possessions and awards and so-called accomplishments will all disappear. What will remain is what matters—but what is that, exactly? I have to figure that out. I cannot easily put my hands around it; I'm growing into it and sometimes I understand it, and that's what makes life meaningful. As Father Luke might summarize, "Live fully in the moment and be content. Work hard, study, but play and rest too. Be quiet, sit down, and listen. And one thing you can do, requiring no one's permission at all to do it, is be self-giving."

ACKNOWLEDGMENTS

My heartfelt thanks go to the many monks who have spent time talking and teaching me over the years. Special thanks to Father Luke and Father Ambrose, to M. Basil Pennington, and Wayne Teasdale. Many thanks, as well, to my editor, Chad Allen.

NOTES

Chapter 1 Changing My Perceptions

1. Thomas Merton, *The Waters of Siloe* (New York: Harcourt, Brace and Company, 1949), xvi.

2. And each is taken from the long out-of-print (and very difficult to find) book, *The Cistercian Sign Language: A Study in Non-verbal Communication*, by Robert A. Barakat (Kalamazoo: Cistercian Publications, 1975).

Chapter 2 The Way of the Camel

1. *The Rule of Saint Benedict*, trans. Abbot Parry OSB (Herefordshire, England: Gracewing, 1990), chapter 6, 23.

2. Friedrich von Hugel, *The Mystical Element of Religion, Vol. 1* (London: J. M. Dent & Sons, 1961), v.

3. *The Habit of Being: Letters of Flannery O'Connor*, ed. Sally Fitzgerald (New York: Farrar, Straus & Giroux, 1988), 354.

4. I talk about this in my book, *Almost Catholic: An Appreciation of the History, Practice, and Mystery of Ancient Faith* (San Francisco: Jossey-Bass, 2008).

5. Ralph Adams Cram, *The Ruined Abbeys of Great Britian* (London: George G. Harrap and Company, n.d.), 282–83.

6. *The Rule of Saint Benedict*, chapter 58, 93.

7. Dean Koontz, *Brother Odd* (New York: Bantam Dell, 2007), 1–2.

Chapter 3 Becoming Real

1. John of the Cross, *The Mystical Doctrine of St. Samuel of the Cross*, ed. R. H. J. Steuart (London: Sheed & Ward, 1934), 174.

2. Thomas Merton, *The Silent Life* (New York: Farrar, Straus & Cudahy, 1957), vii.

3. *The Rule of Saint Benedict*, chapter 38, 66.

4. Michael Leigh Fermor, *A Time to Keep Silence* (New York: New York Review Books, 2007), 10.

5. *The Velveteen Rabbit or How Toys Become Real*, by Margery Williams. First published by Avon Books, New York, 1922.

6. Archbishop Desmond Tutu, foreword to *Anglican Religious Communities Year Book: Fifth International Edition 2006–7* (Norwich, England: Canterbury Press, 2005), vi.

Chapter 4 Friendship and Meaning

1. Fermor, *A Time to Keep Silence*, 55–56.

2. Graham Greene, *A Burnt-Out Case* (New York: Penguin Books, 1968), 151.

3. Laurence Freeman, OSB, "Christian Meditation Newsletter" 31, no. 2 (June 2007), 5.

4. Graham Greene, *The Heart of the Matter* (New York: Penguin Books, 1971), 36.

5. *The Rule of Saint Benedict*, chapter 42, 70.

6. Thomas Merton, *The Monastic Journey*, ed. Brother Michael Hart (Kansas City, MO: Sheed Andrews and McMeel, 1977), 3.

Chapter 5 Sit. Pray. Listen.

1. Freeman, 4.

2. William H. Shannon, *Silent Lamp: The Thomas Merton Story* (New York: Crossroad, 1992), 257.

3. Mgr. Robert Hugh Benson, Preface to *The Life of Saint Teresa*, taken from the French of a Carmelite nun by Alice Lady Lovat (St. Louis: Herder, 1911), xv.

4. Evelyn Underhill, *Concerning the Inner Life* (New York: E. P. Dutton, 1926), 6–7.

5. Compare against Ludwig Wittgenstein, *Tractatus Logico-Philosophicus*, propositions 6.54 and 7. The standard translation is that of D. F. Pears and B. F. McGuinness (Atlantic Highlands, NJ: Humanities Press International, 1974).

6. Leon Bloy, *Pilgrim of the Absolute*, ed. Raissa Maritain, trans. Samuel Coleman and Harry Lorin Binsse (New York: Pantheon Books, 1947), 40.

Chapter 6 Work and Play

1. *The Rule of Saint Benedict*, chapter 7, 62–65.

2. There have been many versions of this prayer, poem, or table grace, since it was originally written by Brigid. This rendering is my own.

Chapter 7 Unlearning Ambition and Originality

1. All quotes from John Cassian's Institutes that follow are from Book X; online translation from The Order of St. Benedict: www.osb.org.

2. John Henry Newman, *Apologia Pro Vita Sua: Being a History of His Religious Opinions* (York: Young and Co, 1881), 195.

3. Thomas Merton, *Conjectures of a Guilty Bystander* (Garden City, NY: Doubleday, 1966), 140–41.

Chapter 8 Life and Death

1. John Henry Newman, *Parochial and Plain Sermons* (Ft. Collins, CO: Ignatius Press, 1997), IV, 22.

2. Heidi F. W. M. de Gouw et al, "Decreased Mortality among Contemplative Monks in The Netherlands," *American Journal of Epidemiology* 141 (1995): 771–75.

3. Muriel Spark, *Memento Mori* (New York: New Directions, 2000), 153.

Chapter 9 Be Home. Love.

1. *The Rule of Saint Benedict* (New York: Penguin Books, 1971), chapter 4, 17–20.

2. Thomas Merton, *Thoughts in Solitude* (New York: Farrar, Straus & Cudahy, 1958), 34–35.

3. Even more recently, *The New York Observer* reported on January 21, 2008, that an editor at Riverhead, a division of Random House's Doubleday book publishing group, paid "more than a million dollars for two books by Mary Samuelson, an acolyte of Mother Teresa's who left the church after 20 years and renounced her faith" (p. 5). Those too will surely sell like hotcakes, but they won't help those outside of faith to understand those inside of it any better than Hitchens and Harris do.

Jon Sweeney has spent many hours and days over the course of two decades with Cistercian monks in Georgia, Kentucky, and Massachusetts. He is the author of many books including *Almost Catholic*, *The St. Francis Prayer Book*, *Born Again and Again*, which was honored with an Award of Merit by *Christianity Today*, and *Light in the Dark Ages*, a History Book Club and Book-of-the-Month Club selection. He lives in Vermont.